Modern Club Swinging
and Pole Spinning

Anna Jillings
of the
Cosmos Jugglers

First Edition

Published by Butterfingers,
Bath, England. April 1994

© 1994 Anna Jillings

All rights reserved

Printed by Redwood Books

ISBN 0 9513240 8 X

A C.I.P. record for this title
is available from the British Library

Acknowledgements

I hope this book will inspire and encourage club swingers and anyone thinking of taking up the skill for the first time. This book presents a series of 20 workshop lessons on club swinging, with reference to manipulating other objects, particularly long poles. The chapters on performance are based on experience as part of the Cosmos Jugglers, FireNoise and from my own solo shows.

I am grateful to many people for their help. My thanks go to: Jim Semlyen; Linda Robson, Mark Tillotson; Rob Stone; Matt Stephens; Ken Zetie; Lara Greene; John Bolwell; Harriet Jillings and Rachel Semlyen for their enthusiasm as well as their helpful editing and suggestions. The illustrations are by Julie Wilson, based on my sketches.

Contents

Introduction

The art of club swinging involves directing the movement of two clubs to form graceful and striking patterns. As well as being very beautiful to watch, this circus and gymnastic skill improves coordination and strengthens the muscles of the shoulders, arms and chest. Swinging is extremely healthy! Club swinging has the added benefits of being creative, stimulating and great fun. Try it and see.

The superb visual appeal of club swinging will probably have encouraged you to read this book. An advantage of this skill is that, although there are many club swinging patterns and combinations, a beginner can become proficient within a relatively short time. It need only take a few months as opposed to years to learn to a good standard. This step-by-step guide assumes no familiarity with the basics of club swinging and movements build in their level of difficulty from simple to more demanding patterns. Selected tricks are also linked to pole spinning which is the naturally related skill of manipulating a long staff.

I discovered club swinging through an interest in juggling. Swinging is a good stretch and warm up before juggling and I found that I enjoyed the unbroken flow of club swinging in comparison to the different challenges involved in keeping many objects in the air during toss juggling. Because there are only two props, it can seem easy compared with other juggling forms and therefore club swinging helps to build confidence.

A Short History of Club Swinging

Modern-day club swinging has its roots in Indian club swinging, which was devised long ago in central Asia. The skill was originally practised as a martial art form. Heavy clubs were swung and used as fast moving weapons for close combat. Indian club swinging was, therefore, first taught as a component of military drill to train warriors and to improve the suppleness of their wrists for fighting.

Club swinging later developed as a way of demonstrating skills and improving fitness. By the turn of the century, pairs of clubs were in common usage in Europe and America as exercise aids. This form of recreation was popular with classes of both sexes and club swinging was once even part of the American core physical education curriculum. The apparatus used then was carved from dense hard woods and old fashioned equipment weighs much more than today's moulded plastic clubs.

As well as improving coordination, the motion of club swinging is of value due to the strength and flexibility it helps to build in the upper body. In particular, full-arm swings will stretch and open up the shoulders and mid back. This is particularly beneficial as these areas are prone to tightness due to every day stress and tension. So, although club swinging is very energetic activity, it can become a relaxing and meditative pastime. There is a soothing aspect to club swinging and small clubs are still sometimes used by physiotherapists to cure mild wrist sprains.

Swinging is usually performed in the clubs' section of the Olympic sport of Modern Rhythmic Gymnastics. Women gymnasts practice with lightweight equipment and their routines often include some extremely high throws. These throws free the hands and body for other movements. Within a short time you should take a risk by occasionally throwing the clubs and thereby integrate toss juggling with your club swinging.

Club swinging was reintroduced to jugglers in America by Michael Moshen and Allan Jacobs. Allan won the US Nationals competition at the 1983 International Juggling Convention with a club swinging and juggling routine, thus inspiring many other jugglers to learn. He is a good teacher as well and his video on club swinging really helped my own technique.

The popularity of club swinging in Europe continues to spread. Swiss performers such as Sören Nossek and Gerda Saxer have influenced the growth of interest in club swinging as a performance skill. In Britain, John Blanchard (Ultravision), Rachel Henson (who trained with the Peking Opera), Marion Kenny, Judy Gouldston and the rhythmic gymnast, juggler and dancer Kati Ylä-Hokkala (of the Gandini Project) all use intricate club swinging movements in their shows.

Fire Swinging

Fire torch swinging in the dark is extremely attractive. To the onlooker, someone swinging with fire appears to burn rounded pathways in the darkness behind the torches. This effect was my main motivation to learn club swinging. At that time, I was performing with the Oxford fire troupe FireNoise. The show needed reliable and dramatic routines and our group fire swinging provided a wonderful spectacle.

When you start using fire, safety should be always of paramount concern. I include a chapter dedicated to the use of fire that gives advice on the correct fuel and essential procedures for outdoor fire practice and performance (pages 80 - 82).

Ultraviolet Light

Safer, but just as dramatic and impressive as fire is the use of ultraviolet (uv) or black light, with fluorescent and luminous equipment. Moving trails can be given different colours and the effect produced can be quite magical. I include hints on how to perform with this medium on pages 86 - 88. You need an audience to appreciate uv and soon you will find yourself in demand.

How To Use This Book

This book is a workshop guide to club swinging, with sections on the closely related skill of pole spinning.

Although this is not an advanced text, readers will have to concentrate to follow the instructions given. This is partly as a result of the inherent difficulties of attempting to write down a dynamic movement skill on paper. You may have to study sections more than once and have the equipment at hand before you can follow a workshop lesson. However, if you find a good sized space to practice regularly and persevere, then your efforts will be rewarded.

When learning indoors you will need about 4 to 5 feet in head room above the place where you swing and also to remove all easily breakable objects from the room. Outdoor practice is invigorating in good weather. Many people find that playing music with a strong rhythm improves the energy and fun of a practice session.

Important summary directions are in large, bold print and indented from the margin.

Different sizes of text are designed to make it easier to read the instructions from a distance. You will learn faster if you prop this book open and read the bold directions while standing with the equipment.

Diagrams have broken lines to indicate the paths of the clubs in a complete movement. These path lines are dashed for the right hand club. For the left hand, lines with alternating dots and dashes mark the club's trail. Lines are dotted when the path of the swing travels behind the person in the figure. Arrows are used to show the direction of the movement.

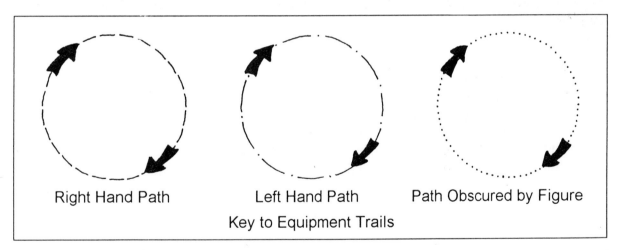

Right Hand Path   Left Hand Path   Path Obscured by Figure

Key to Equipment Trails

Notice that the mirror image is presented when you check your reflection and that the sides in this book's figures are swapped.

Every circle has a twin circle that is made in the opposite direction. Your club swinging will be much more impressive and adaptable if you aspire to learn movements in all directions.

Always aim to make precise and symmetrical club swinging patterns with your arms straight.

You are strongly advised to watch yourself practising in a mirror since this is the best way to check if your body and patterns are in line. Whilst large mirrors are not always available a substitute is any reflective surface, such as glass. Mirrors are invaluable when putting together a routine as they will allow you to see which transitional moves can be used to link the separate movements together into a flowing sequence.

Because a person's concentration span tends to be quite short, it will be best to work through this book in modest sections. If you come across problems, then refer to the chapter on overcoming difficulties on pages 75 - 77. Every now and then, review the material that you have learnt by looking back at earlier sections.

When you have grasped a new pattern you could teach it to a friend. If they are interested, you will have someone to practise with and this leads to faster progress. In particular, verbal explanations will clarify the defining features of a pattern and this can enable you to adapt it with your own variations. A tip is to make notes on your personally devised tricks and there is space to do this at the end of this book. Notes will help in remembering your own moves later and serve as proof of your advancement. Choreographed swinging in groups is very entertaining - teach enough people and you will soon have a performance troupe.

As well as learning with the aid of this guide, ask others to show you what they know and use your own imagination to create new patterns

Be kind to yourself when learning to club swing. Warm up and use lightweight clubs with soft plastic bodies to minimise the danger from hitting yourself with a club. Suggested warm up exercises are given in the following pages. Take regular breaks and be mindful of your limits with this deceptively physical exercise. Remember also that if you want to improve, there is absolutely no substitute for practice. **Good luck.**

Club Swinging Summary

- Warm up, particularly the shoulders and wrists.
- Fully stretch out the arms and keep the clubs exactly in line.
- Allow gravity and the momentum of the swinging clubs to help the motion.
- Swing perfectly rounded circles.
- Straighten patterns by looking in a mirror.
- Swing close to the body and keep the wrists touching in follow time.
- Learn patterns with both hands in all directions to achieve true symmetry.
- Work on smooth transitions.

Warming Up Before Swinging

Warming up is an essential aspect of safely learning to club swing. Although it is tempting to go straight to the equipment, invest in a short time to loosen up before any practice session and you will gain the benefits in terms of:

- Faster progress
- Reduced chances of sprains and strains
- Greater reach and suppleness
- Better tonality of the ligaments and muscles
- Improved fitness

Moving without the clubs is worthwhile, since it focuses on the basic pre-requisite of graceful swinging - *flexibility.*

Wear loose and comfortable clothing. Put on extra layers for warming up and prepare by standing with your feet a few inches apart and arms by your sides in a relaxed stance. Take all the exercises at a slow pace to avoid straining the muscles when cold.

Arm Exercises
Forward Direction
Start with your right arm reaching up above your head. Swing the arm to the front and down. Continue the arc so that the arm rises behind and completes a full circle. You are tracing a large circle, with the shoulder at its centre. Repeat 4 times with each arm. Lastly, alternate both arms so that they are half a cycle apart like swimming a stroke called the 'front crawl,' except the elbow should not bend.

Backward Direction
Start with your arms at your sides. Swing the right hand up and to the front of you until it is reaching straight up in the air. Continue to arc backwards until you have completed a full circle. Repeat this swing 4 times. Next, swing 4 backward circles with the left arm alone. Finally, try swinging left and right arms so that they are a half cycle apart and alternating - as though you were swimming backstroke.

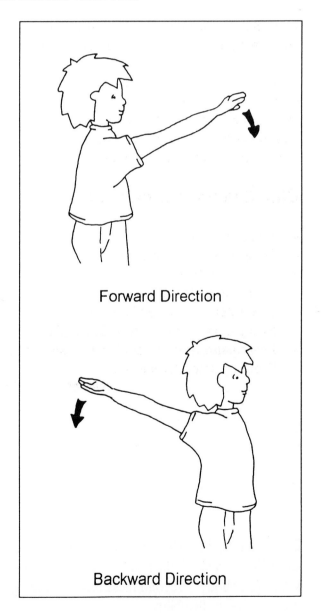

Forward Direction

Backward Direction

Outward Direction

Lift the right arm so that it is outstretched horizontally. Swing the arm down, in front of the body, up the left side and past your face. The palm begins facing down and during the move the palm turns towards the body as it passes the body. Repeat 4 times, then swap to the left hand and then do this move with both arms together.

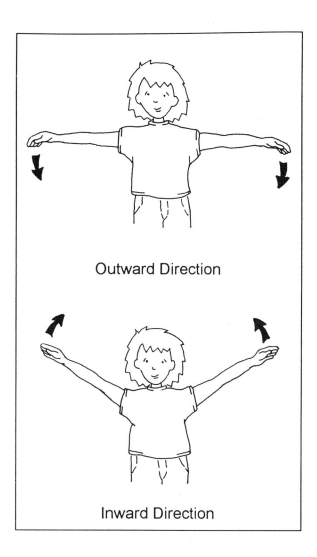

Outward Direction

Inward Direction

Inward Direction

Lift the right arm to the horizontal on the right side of the body. Continue raising the arm up and towards the head, with the right arm beginning to fall only once it is over to the left side. Thus, you trace out a circle in front of the body in the opposite direction to before. Repeat 4 times. Swap arms and lastly, swing both arms together simultaneously.

Shoulder Exercises

Roll the right shoulder forward 4 times. Try this backward, then in both directions with the left shoulder.
Rotate both shoulders backward together. Do this forward too.

Elbow Exercises

Raise and bend your right arm so that the elbow is pointing up in the air and then rest your right hand behind your right shoulder. Gently use the left hand to ease the elbow further back. Repeat using the left arm.
Interlock the fingers of both hands and then stretch out the arms in front of you with the palms pushing away. Still with the fingers linked, circle the arms both to the left and right.

Wrist Exercises

With both hands, shake out your wrists and then clench your fists. Repeat 4 times.
Stretch out your hands and wiggle all your fingers.
With the arms outstretched, rotate the hands in the air at the wrist, in both directions. Shake your wrists to release any remaining tension.

Exercises for the Rest of the Body

Look over each shoulder and make small circles with your head to conclude a loosening of your upper body. Beyond these basics, rotating the hips, knees and ankles is recommended for complete body flexibility.

6

Lesson 1
Full-Arm Circles

By swinging from your shoulders with your arms fully stretched, you will be able to create patterns with a very wide circumference. These form the largest swinging patterns. They are extremely visual and yet are some of the easiest moves to learn.

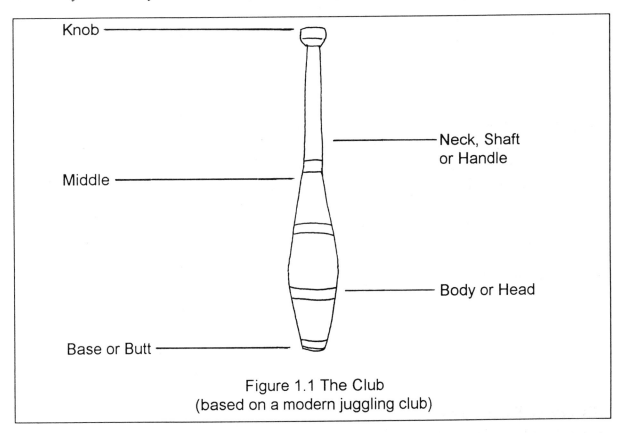

Knob

Neck, Shaft or Handle

Middle

Body or Head

Base or Butt

Figure 1.1 The Club
(based on a modern juggling club)

If you do not yet have two clubs, see the chapter on equipment on pages 89 - 90 for varieties of clubs. Clubs can be bought from any juggling retailer and selected sports shops.

Different kinds of grip are used on the club and these are introduced as needed. Full-arm circle movements use a solid grip.

Solid Grip
Hold the knob of the club with your thumb and first two fingers.

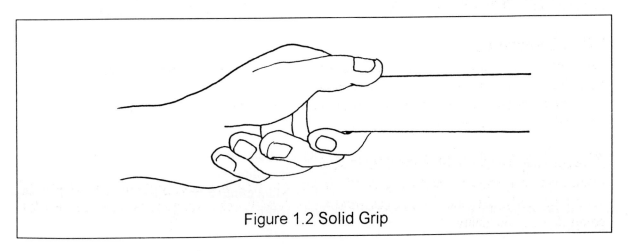

Figure 1.2 Solid Grip

It is as though you were shaking hands with the very top of the thinnest part of the club. Do not place the knob of the club in between your first two fingers because it is difficult to change grip and, eventually, the misplacement will cause the knob to rub against your skin with possible blistering. Figure 1.3 shows the correct placement of the knob.

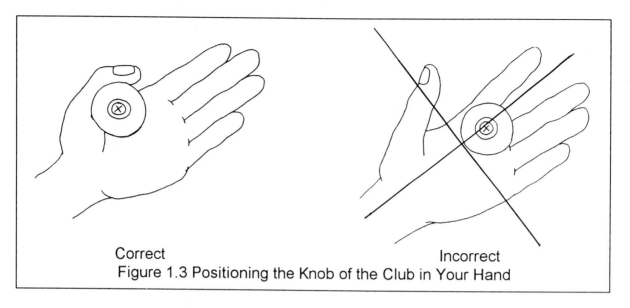

Correct   Incorrect
Figure 1.3 Positioning the Knob of the Club in Your Hand

Starting Position

Take up a fairly closed stance with the clubs held straight upright in front of you and with arms slightly bent. It is from this motionless position that the swinger has maximum control.

Stand tall and arch the chest to enhance breathing. Hold the clubs upright as shown in Figure 1.4.

Whenever you try a new pattern just do one round at first and then return to the starting position. Once you have the feel of the movement, build up to performing several cycles in succession ending with a neat stop at the same starting position.

Figure 1.4 Starting Position

The crucial aspect of this position is that the clubs are held upright at chest level. The feet can be either slightly apart or kept together. If you discipline yourself to stand in the starting position to gather concentration before and after completing a move then it will become a natural point of orientation. The stance is very useful control position for beginning new directions or timings.

Two Vertical Directions

Circles can be made in a variety of sizes and directions. This lesson teaches full-arm circles in the vertical plane, sometimes known as the "wall plane" (because it is vertical like the walls of a room). The directions will be familiar from the warm up section on pages 5 - 6. If you have skipped over the proposed warm ups, at least flex your upper body and shoulders before attempting the following movements. This is particularly recommended if you are unaccustomed to club swinging, otherwise you may suffer slight muscle strain.

The figure below shows a plan view looking down on a club swinger. The dashed lines indicate vertical planes that are behind and in front of the person and you should aim to trace circles with the base of the club against these imaginary vertical planes.

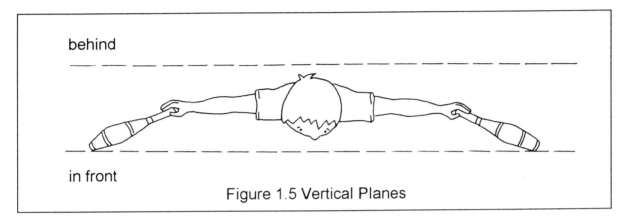

behind

in front

Figure 1.5 Vertical Planes

Outward Direction

From starting position, raise both hands up and away from the head. The right club travels right and the left club travels left. Swing down, crossing hands low and back to the start. Figure 1.6.

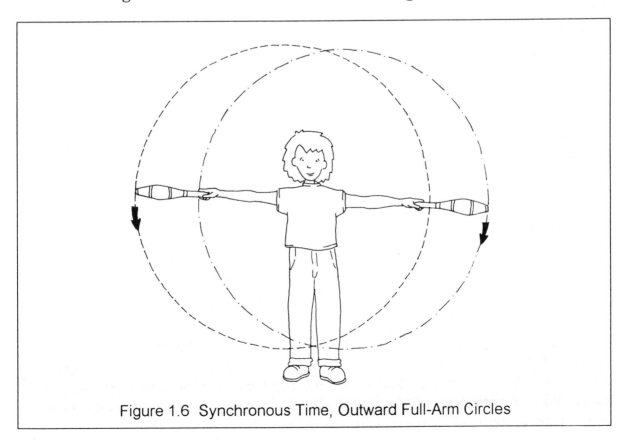

Figure 1.6 Synchronous Time, Outward Full-Arm Circles

Trace one full-arm circle (sometimes called large-arm), with both arms extended and your shoulder at the centre of the circle. Stop neatly at the starting position. Repeat 4 times. Once you have the feel of the outward direction, continue to swing several circles in succession.

Look down one arm at a time and hold the equipment as though the clubs were an extension of your arms. Even in advanced swinging forms when the clubs are thrown, they should always remain at the same angle as the arms. Clubs are badly positioned if they break with the line of the arms either upward or by dipping downward.

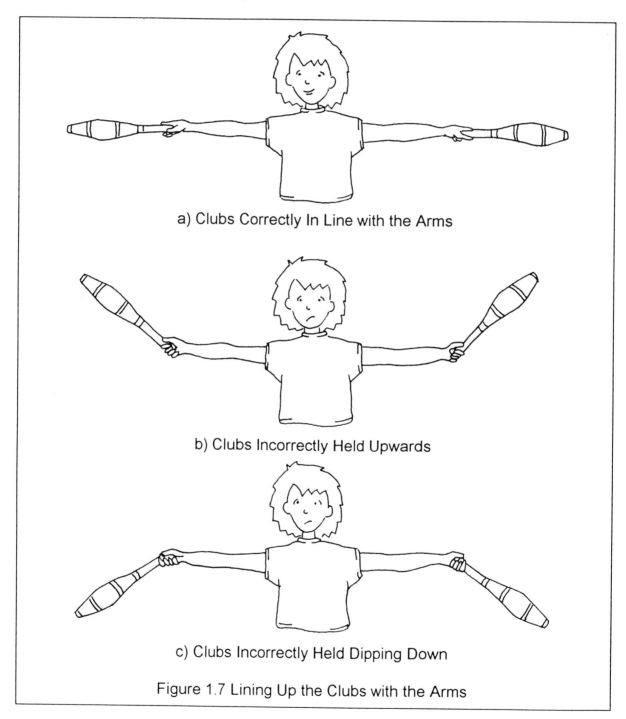

a) Clubs Correctly In Line with the Arms

b) Clubs Incorrectly Held Upwards

c) Clubs Incorrectly Held Dipping Down

Figure 1.7 Lining Up the Clubs with the Arms

Inward Direction

Raise both hands up and toward the head. The right club arcs left and the left club arcs right. Swing down, crossing one hand over the other above the head. Figure 1.8b (middle picture opposite).

10

With the right hand crossing over the left (or vice versa), trace out a circle in front of the body inward which is the opposite direction to outward. Try to prevent the clubs from knocking, but do not worry if this direction seems awkward at first. Many people find inward circles more difficult than outward, so repeat the inward movement until it begins to feel increasingly comfortable.

Club swinging patterns are created by combining various timings and directions. The most popular class of movements is to draw out the same circle with both hands. This is called synchronous time and is what you have used in the section above. Other basic patterns for full-arm circles are alternating time and moves in parallel.

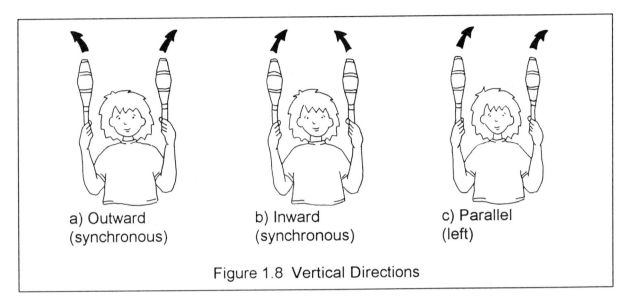

a) Outward
(synchronous)

b) Inward
(synchronous)

c) Parallel
(left)

Figure 1.8 Vertical Directions

Synchronous Time (or same time): Both hands move at the same time, simultaneously, in a single direction (e.g., both inward).

Alternating Time: The circular movements made by your clubs succeed each other in turns. This is an off-synch timing in which the clubs swing precisely half a revolution apart, usually in a single direction (e.g., outward, alternating circles).

Parallel: Hands move together, continually side by side. One hand takes one direction, and the other follows its path so that the clubs remain the same distance apart (often shoulder width) at all points. Clubs can travel either in parallel to the left or to the right and true parallel time requires the swinger to have equally good control over both outward and inward directions.

Use a mirror to check the symmetry of your patterns. Practise the above timings and directions and you will have learnt a total of six, full-arm club swinging patterns on the vertical front plane. Using the starting position to begin and end all movements, swing a short routine with 4 each of:

1. Synchronous outward full-arm circles;
2. Synchronous inward full-arm circles;
3. Alternating outward full-arm circles;
4. Alternating inward full-arm circles;
5. Parallel right full-arm circles;
6. Parallel left full-arm circles.

Lesson 2
Forward and Backward Full-Arm Circles and a Pirouette

This lesson explores movements performed in the vertical plane with the swinger facing side on to the audience. This vertical plane sideways is parallel to the two dotted lines passing through the shoulders of the person in Figure 2.1, viewed from above. The new plane is at right angles to the plane that we have thus far used, those shown as dashed lines both in front and behind the body. Turn yourself sideways to perform forward or backward moves as it is only from the side that a proper view is presented of full circles.

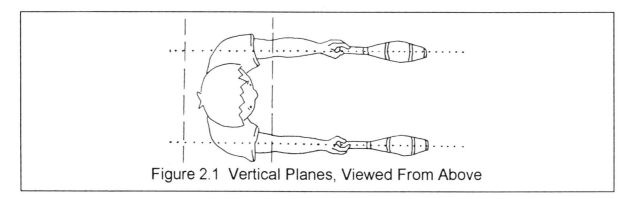

Figure 2.1 Vertical Planes, Viewed From Above

Symmetry is a very important aspect of achieving good club swinging arcs. The vertical planes are also described in Figure 2.2 below, in which the swinger stands in the centre of a space where two planes cross at an angle of exactly 90 degrees.

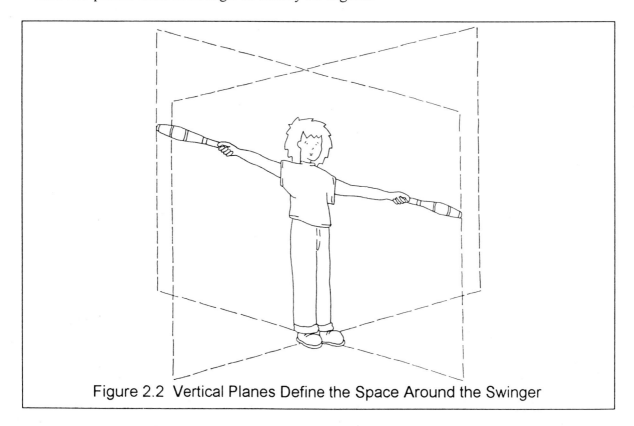

Figure 2.2 Vertical Planes Define the Space Around the Swinger

Full-Arm Circles Forward

For all the following movements you must hold each club in a solid grip (Figure 1.2 on page 7 shows a solid grip). With each arm in turn, swing forward circles taking care that the arm and club are held straight and in a perfect line.

12

One hand reaches straight up. Swing the arm to the front and down, then back to a high position above the head. Repeat 4 times and with the other hand.

Swing full-arm circles in alternating time - like swimming the crawl, but with your elbows always straight. Figure 2.3.

When swinging alternating full-arm circles, you may find it easier if you allow your body to twist slightly. Watch sideways in a mirror and your arms should seem to be connected as though they were a straight stick. Try walking forwards or backwards while performing this alternating time move.

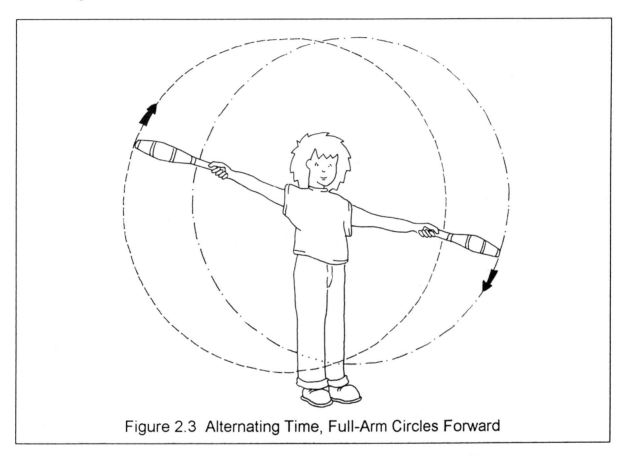

Figure 2.3 Alternating Time, Full-Arm Circles Forward

The anatomy of the shoulder does not allow the behind-the-back part of the move to be done with both hands at once and synchronous time circles will feel uncomfortable unless you allow your arms to reach out to the sides.

Full-Arm Circles Backward

The opposite of the previous move is to swing full-arm circles in the backward direction. This direction was explained in the warm up chapter on page 5.

Lift one hand up to the front of you until it is reaching straight up in the air. Continue upwards in the direction of swimming backstroke. Repeat 4 times and swap hands.

Alternating time full-arm circles backward.

Try moving around your practice space while swinging full-arm alternating moves. Improve your coordination by synchronizing your arms and legs, either together or in alternating time.

Adding A Pirouette

It is possible to turn your body on the spot from swinging an alternating full-arm pattern on the side vertical plane. The feet do most of the turning, while the arms help the momentum of the whole body spin.

Begin alternating full-arm circles forward. As one club is approaching its lowest point, turn the feet around one half turn towards it. Notice that the arms are now making backward circles. Complete the turn by following a high backward club around.
Lastly, try a full pirouette.

Tips for this one are relax and go slowly. Pretty soon, your arms won't feel as if they are flailing wildly and you will have mastered a neat turning full-arm pirouette.

Prepare for a turn by standing with your feet crossed. The straight leg makes the turn by spinning on the ball of the foot while the other foot acts to steady the pirouette. Take a rest if you begin to get dizzy. Alternatively, a technique called "spotting" can help avoid disorientation. Spotting involves focusing on a distant point until the last possible instant of a pirouette. Then, quickly whip your head around and regain your concentration on that spot.

Opposition Time with Forward and Backward Full-Arm Circles

Opposition timing is a useful transitional move as well as a real coordination teaser.

Opposition Time: One arm circles forward, while at the same time the other arm is swung in the backward direction.

Start with both arms straight up in the air. One full-arm circle goes forward and the other backward, synchronously and in perfect opposition - Figure 2.4. Arms pass each other at the highest and lowest positions. Stop high and then swap sides.

The essence of this timing is that the two arms should always be doing exactly opposite moves. So, if you notice that both arms are going in the same direction (either both forward or backward), stop and start again.

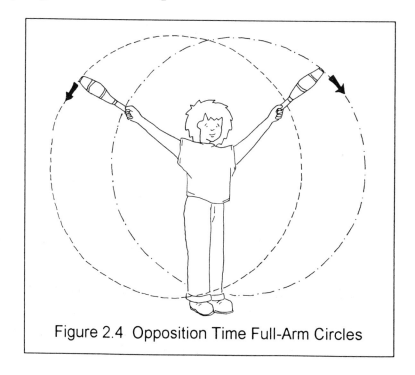

Figure 2.4 Opposition Time Full-Arm Circles

Lesson 3
Forward and Backward Hand Circles

Continuing from Lesson 2's exploration of full-arm patterns seen from the side, this lesson introduces two complementary moves - forward and backward hand circles. Hand circles have a much smaller circumference than the full-arm circle and they will add variety to your club swinging. A hand circle has a radius equal to the length of the club and pivots around the wrist joint. These patterns predominantly use the ring grip and look best if the swing is kept flat and as close to your arm as possible.

Ring Grip

Put the knob of the club in the notch between your thumb and first finger and loosely make a ring, allowing the club enough play to rotate freely. Figures 3.1 and 3.2.

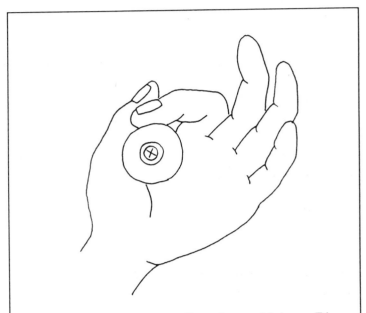

Figure 3.1 Thumb and Forefinger Make a Ring Around the Club Knob

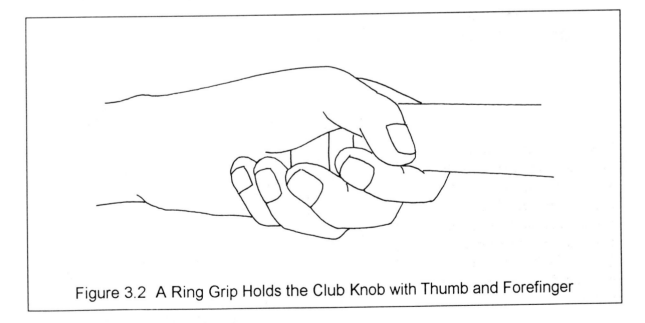

Figure 3.2 A Ring Grip Holds the Club Knob with Thumb and Forefinger

Forward Hand Circles Outside the Arms

With clubs held in a ring grip, begin making small circles to the front with your wrist at the centre. Hold your arms horizontal, at chest level and shoulder-width apart. The clubs swing on the outside of the arms with elbows slightly bent, as if you were turning a skipping rope.

With a single club in a ring grip, swing forward hand circles outside that arm. Repeat and swap hands. With both hands, make synchronous forward hand circles directly in front, at chest level. Figure 3.3.

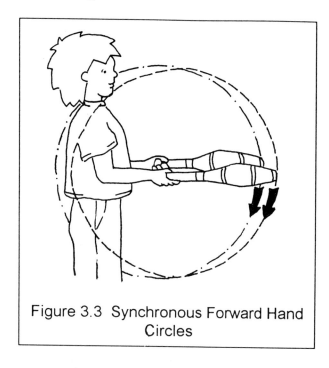

Figure 3.3 Synchronous Forward Hand Circles

Synchronous time forward hand circles feel like skipping. Try adding a little bounce to your knees to aid your sense of rhythm. The clubs should pass perpendicularly outside the arms, i.e., parallel to the arms, again flat to the vertical or "wall plane." This class of pattern look good when seen from the side as only from this angle is a full circle visible.

Alternating time forward hand circles.

For all alternating time patterns the aim is to keep two circles exactly half a revolution apart. This takes some practice as you will need to learn how to keep both hands' circuits turning at precisely the same speed. Learn a new timing by swinging circles with just the weaker hand (the left hand if you are right handed) and then bring in your stronger hand to make opposite sides of the pattern swing out of synch. Start practising alternating time at a slow speed and then build up the control to go faster. It may help to count a rhythm out loud to yourself 1.2 1.2. 1.2, with one circle peaking on 1 and the other reaching its peak on the count of 2.

Hand circle movements in alternating time are initially difficult to sustain. Add variety as, for instance, it looks great when the swinger changes the position of a standard pattern by raising the clubs high above the head and then lowers the clubs to the ground.

Backward Hand Circles Outside the Arms
Clubs are again held in a ring grip and these moves involve hand circles swinging backward.

Synchronous backward hand circles at chest level.
Alternating time backward hand circles outside the arms.

The first pattern is similar to skipping backwards. Learn to stop the clubs neatly and to go from forwards to backwards and back at will, with both hands. I find that it is easiest to stop at either of the two points when the club is parallel to the floor, on the horizontal plane - see Figure 3.4 opposite. Gain further control by isolating the movements of each hand and changing the direction of one hand independently from the other.

Stop Near the Body   Stop Away from the Body

Figure 3.4 Horizontal Stopping Positions for Forward and Backward Hand Circles

Opposition Time Hand Circles Outside the Arms

One side circles forward and the other backward, in opposition.

From starting position, make synchronous time hand circles turn in different directions, e.g. with the right hand going forward while the left rotates backward. Figure 3.5. Stop neatly, change directions and repeat the move with circles always moving in opposition.

This pattern took me many attempts. I could master the control only after a lot of effort had been put into strengthening my weaker left wrist.

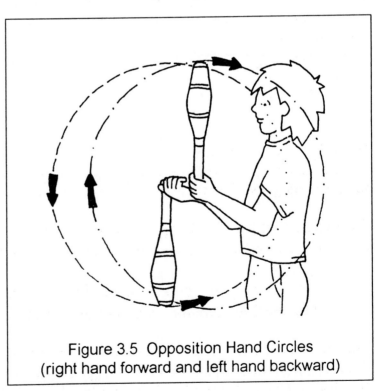

Figure 3.5 Opposition Hand Circles
(right hand forward and left hand backward)

Lesson 4
Two Front Facing Hand Circles with the Ring Grip

Two further positions for hand circles made with the ring grip are lower-front and shoulder (or upper-back hand) circles. Like the full-arm circles in Lesson 1, these patterns are most clearly seen from a front view.

Lower-Front Hand Circles
Let your right arm hang straight down with the hand at hip level. Make outward lower-front hand circles using a ring grip. Figure 4.1.

Watch that the rotation of the club makes a full circle rather than an oval and try to keep the arm straight and still, allowing the wrist alone to swing the club. Remember to hold the club loosely.

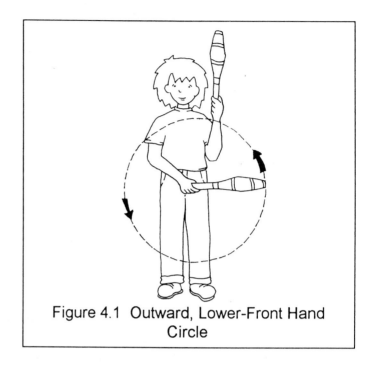

Figure 4.1 Outward, Lower-Front Hand Circle

Having begun a circle, a ring grip should provide flexibility so that the club turns with the aid of gravity and so you need just put in enough energy to keep it going and direct its curved path. Although this will feel awkward at first, a limber wrist will develop in time. Swap hands and repeat the outward movement.

> **Both hands with clubs in the ring grip. Swing synchronous, outward lower-front hand circles with the hands kept far enough apart to avoid knocking the clubs.**

Practise these synchronous circles until they feel comfortable. Watch yourself in a mirror checking that both circles are flat to the front vertical wall plane.

> **Outward, lower-front hand circles in alternating time.**

Aim to keep alternating circles exactly half a revolution apart. Now for these circles inward.

> **Try the lower-front circle in the inward direction with one hand only and then with two clubs synchronously and in alternating time.**

It is important to recognise that every club swinging spin can be made in **at least** two directions. *Every circle has its opposite number or twin.* Throughout this guide, I usually teach the outward direction first as it has the most natural feel. However, spend at least as much time, if not more, learning inward circles. The effort will be worthwhile since you will be better balanced, particularly when performing moves in parallel and when building up routines.

Parallel lower-fronts, both to the right and left (clockwise and anti - clockwise as seen from the swinger's viewpoint). Figure 4.2.

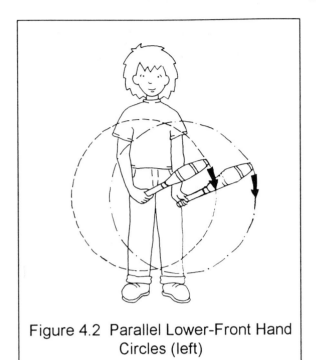

Figure 4.2 Parallel Lower-Front Hand Circles (left)

Try all the above lower-front circle moves with your **elbow** as the central pivot joint instead of your wrist, i.e., synchronous, alternating and parallel elbow circles.

Elbow circles provide a medium sized circle but they are less commonly used than the other two sizes (full-arm and small hand circles). This is because elbows have limited flexibility and elbow circles are really only possible to the front at mid height.

Shoulder Circles, (or Upper-Back Hand Circles)

In general, the names of patterns suggest their position. Shoulder circles are performed high and at the back of the body. They are sometimes called upper-back hand circles. These movements are made with the wrist as the pivotal centre point and with the club held in the ring grip.

With one hand, begin making forward hand circles in front (Figure 3.1). Slowly move the arm out to the side of the body, with the elbow slightly bent. Let the club fall behind the arm and towards the head. Continue the motion, making one full hand circle in the upper-back position going outward. Figure 4.3.

Try shoulder circles with each hand individually, building up to rotate for 8 counts. Do not lean backwards when you first try these patterns.

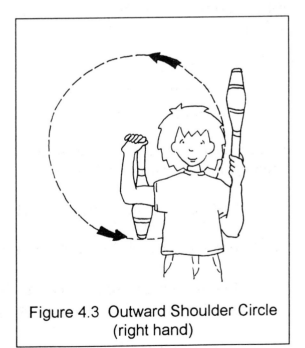

Figure 4.3 Outward Shoulder Circle (right hand)

Outward, synchronous time shoulder circles.

Go slowly at first, being careful not to hit your head or to knock the clubs together at the back. Attempt to make these circles as flat and as close to your arm as possible. They look best in the vertical or "wall plane" that is immediately behind the body. Move on to attempting the inward direction with shoulder circles. From starting position:

Lift one hand to the side of the body with the elbow slightly bent, like the position of the hand in Figure 4.3. Raise the club up and towards the head by flexing the wrist using the ring grip. Allow the club to swing down and back to complete a full shoulder circle inwards, behind your body.

This is the opposite direction to outward shoulder circles and should be attempted slowly at first. Check the planes so that the club makes a flat pattern as close to the arm as you can.

Inward shoulder circles with one hand only and then with both hands in synchronous time.

Well done. Now for the most difficult move of this lesson. First mime parallel shoulder circles by pretending to perform the move without clubs. This is useful to gain an idea of the coordinated wrist action needed. Next hold the clubs upright in a wide starting position.

Parallel time, shoulder circles left and right. Figure 4.4.

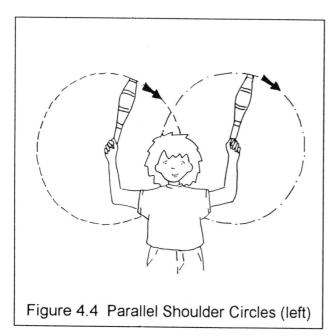

Figure 4.4 Parallel Shoulder Circles (left)

A tip for controlling this move is to start with hands spaced a little apart, so that the clubs are less likely to collide. Do not spend long attempting parallel shoulder circles if you are finding them problematic. However, I believe that trying the parallel every now and then is worthwhile since both inward and outward directions should be equally developed.

You have probably noticed that high patterns are more tiring to perform than moves lower down. This is due to the extra effort involved in raising the weight of both the arm and club. When your arms begin to feel heavy, switch to a more restful lower-front or full-arm pattern. Always stop if you get any cramp or pain in the hands, shake out tension and rest for a while.

Continue to check your reflection whenever you are practising. This is the best way to produce perfectly rounded patterns that have a pleasing symmetry in line with the planes of your body.

Lesson 5
Combining Full-Arm with Hand Circles

Moves that incorporate a mixture of different sized circles are more interesting than single ratio movements (patterns with constant radius). The attraction lies in variety, an element of surprise, and in the slightly higher level of coordination skills and rhythm required to perform linked patterns.

Smooth Combinations

To create a series of flowing movements, large and small circles must swing in the same direction. So, for instance, if you have set in motion an *outward* full-arm swing, it feels much more harmonious to incorporate an *outward* hand circle than an inward move. When you decide to change the basic direction of a pattern, for now, the easiest method is to briefly return to the starting position to make the adjustment. With practice, you will be able to link smooth combinations with transitional moves.

Rhythm

A complete, full-arm circle normally takes twice as long as a small hand circle. Because the timing is different, successfully incorporating two types of circles requires a sense of rhythm. Counting time out loud is a useful aid to coordinating your arms. Playing music that has a strong beat as you practise will also enhance your own rhythm and add to your enjoyment.

Full-Arm and Lower-Front Circles in Synchronous Time

From starting position, begin an outward full-arm circle on count 1, adding an outward lower-front circle on count 2 and completing the full-arm circle on count 3.

Next for the combination move with both hands, Figure 5.1.

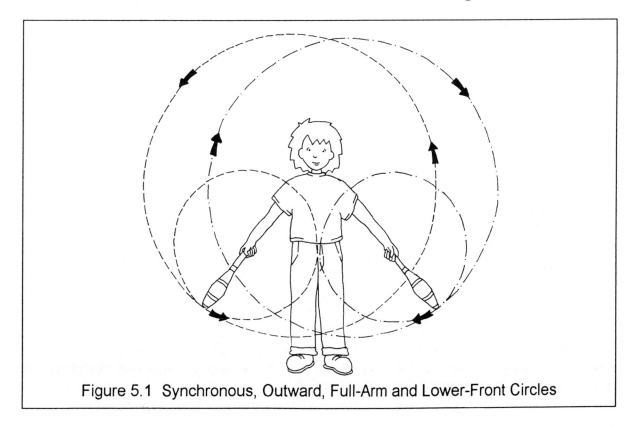

Figure 5.1 Synchronous, Outward, Full-Arm and Lower-Front Circles

Notice that synchronous time, lower-front circles must be kept a little apart to prevent collisions. Practise completing combinations with just one of each type of circle initially, then double up circles to make patterns in double time.

Double Time: All circles are performed twice.

> **Double up circles by performing each circle twice.**
> **Swing the previous patterns in the inward direction.**

Repeating a circle twice requires more concentration and control than a single revolution. This is true for all coordination skills. For instance, jugglers will know that continuous tricks take longer to perfect than a solitary trick.

Parallel Combinations

> **From starting position, swing the clubs in parallel full-arm circles left, adding parallel lower-front circles on the second count.**
> **Double up all circles (2 arm circles followed by 2 hand circles).**
> **Change direction from the starting position to parallels right.**

Attempt to keep these parallel moves shoulder width apart. At no stage do the clubs touch and both arms should be moving at exactly the same speed.

To spice up your parallel moves, how about taking side steps in time with the full-arm arc, either left or right? Travelling with the pattern involves linking both the arms and the steps. Do this to music and you will begin to dance with your club swinging. This will greatly raise the level of your skill, although take care to avoid hitting your shins.

Alternating Time Combinations

> **From starting position, the weaker hand begins an outward full-arm and lower-front hand circle combination. When this is flowing, add the stronger side in alternating time by starting a full-arm outward circle just as the weaker hand begins its lower-front circle.**

Alternating, or off-synch, timing may take a little while to find. Always practise the movement first with your less dominant hand (the left hand if you are right handed) This gives the weaker side more exercise and will help to strengthen it so that, eventually, both sides are equally adept. After the movement is mastered with one hand, introduce the other and, finally, use both so that circles remain a half cycle apart.

A tip is to stretch out when completing the full-arm movement with the elbow straight. The full-arm swing will then leave enough time for a neat hand circle. There's no need to hurry. Next try:

> **Inward, alternating time, full-arm and lower-front circles.**

Never skip the inward move as a true balance in your swinging requires conscious effort, even self-discipline to learn moves in **both directions**. Eventually, patterns will become smooth and you will be able to change directions and timing with an even-sided grace and beauty.

Full-Arm and Shoulder Circles in Synchronous Time

With one hand, begin a single outward full-arm circle. Once it has gained momentum, add a single outward shoulder circle.

Then try with both hands to swing synchronous time, full-arm and shoulder circles. Figure 5.2.

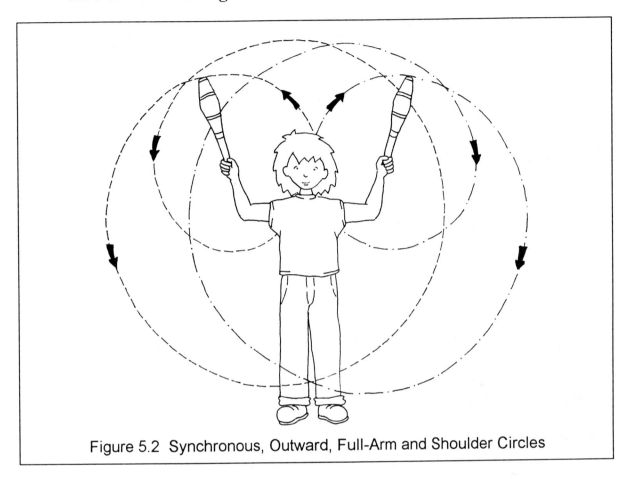

Figure 5.2 Synchronous, Outward, Full-Arm and Shoulder Circles

The arms are outstretched for most of the full-arm circle, except when dipping into the shoulder circle. Then the elbow bends to sink the club behind the shoulder and towards the nape of the neck.

The arms will cross at front chest level and so you must decide whether to swing the right wrist over the left or vice versa. A worthwhile exercise is to change between placing the left hand and then right hand on top. Next for the inward combinations:

Inward, synchronous time full-arm and shoulder circles.
Double up all circles.

The inward, synchronous time involves the arms crossing twice - they pass once above the head and then again at waist level. At neither point should the clubs knock against each other. If they do, then check the symmetry of your pattern in a mirror. It is likely that your weaker hand is tracing circles that are uneven against the wall plane (they will look oval rather than round). The solution is to work the weaker hand in isolation before re-attempting an improved synchronous time pattern.

Parallel Time: Parallel combinations of full-arm and shoulder circles are attractive. Try some now. You will find more comprehensive advice in Lesson 12.

Alternating Time: This very popular move is known as the reel. It is explored in detail in Lesson 6.

Combining Three Circles In A Series

Linking all the positions for circles that we have covered in this lesson will enable you to create an impressive club swinging sequence. It's up to you how many of each type of swing you add in any combination. The most attractive moves will be those that retain symmetry and a smooth sense of rhythm.

Try a synchronous time, outward combination of all three circles, i.e., full-arm, lower-front and shoulder circles.

There are the options of varying:

- direction;
- timing;
- doubling up any, or all circles;
- swinging one arm in isolation.

Short Practice Routine

The following routine begins at starting position, Figure 1.4. Most music has four beats to the bar, so you should repeat each swing four times.

1. Both hands, synchronised, outward full-arm circles.
2. Synchronised outward, full-arm and lower-front circle combination.
3. Synchronised outward, full-arm and shoulder circle combination.
4. Stop at starting position to begin synchronous time, inward full-arm circles.
5. Briefly stop just one hand to go into alternating time inward full-arm circles.
6. Stop at start position then make parallel full-arm circles left.
7. Parallel left elbow circles, (medium sized circles with the elbow at the centre).
8. Parallel left lower-front hand circles, up with half a full-arm circle to finish with clubs held high.

Lesson 6
The Popular Reel and Alternating Timing

A reel is the name of a class of club swinging patterns in alternating time. The most popular reel combines outward, full-arm and shoulder circles swung off-synch. This move feels great to perform as it relaxes and opens up the shoulders. Once learnt, the rhythm will seem natural and the pattern can be done impressively fast!

First with your weaker hand only, swing outward combinations of full-arm and shoulder circles. The stronger side then finds the alternating time by starting the outward swing as the other club begins to rise from the lowest point of its full-arm circle. Figure 6.1.

Your elbows should bend into the shoulder circle, but be locked straight for the full-arm circle so that they form a big, outwards stretch. Bouncing a little with your knees can sometimes help to establish the rhythm. Once you have the beginnings of the move, check the symmetry of your pattern in a mirror.

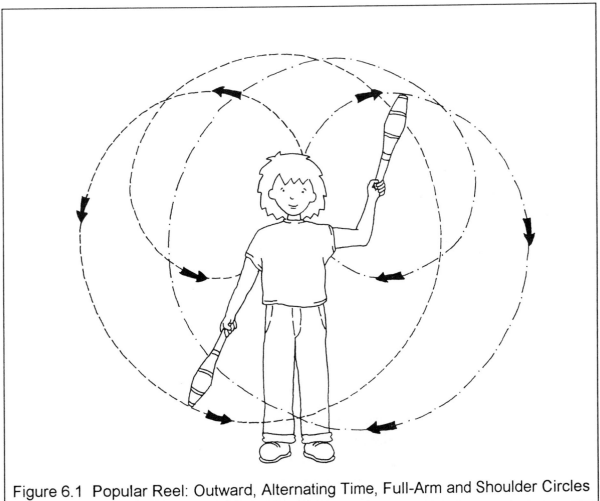

Figure 6.1 Popular Reel: Outward, Alternating Time, Full-Arm and Shoulder Circles

To learn any alternating time move, start with your weaker side and only bring in the stronger side to find the true rhythm. If you are right handed, exercise the left side most because this will improve your ambidexterity, finally leading to perfect swinging form.

25

Forward and backward hand circles in opposition time (Lesson 3, page 17) can be linked in combination with a popular reel making an interesting sequence that involves twisting your body to perform the opposition side spins.

Of course, the popular reel can be done in the opposite direction - i.e., inward.

Weak hand alone, inward combination full-arm and shoulder circles. Other side joins pattern in alternating time.

It may help to turn your hips slightly as you try the inwards reel. The wrist action needed for an inward shoulder circle is similar to that used for a fast serve in the game of tennis.

Reels with a Long Pole

The popular reel is an extremely effective move with a pole. Use an ordinary broomstick as these are strong, cheap and available from any hardware shop. First pick up a pole and hold its centre loosely in the notch between your thumb and first finger, Figure 6.2.

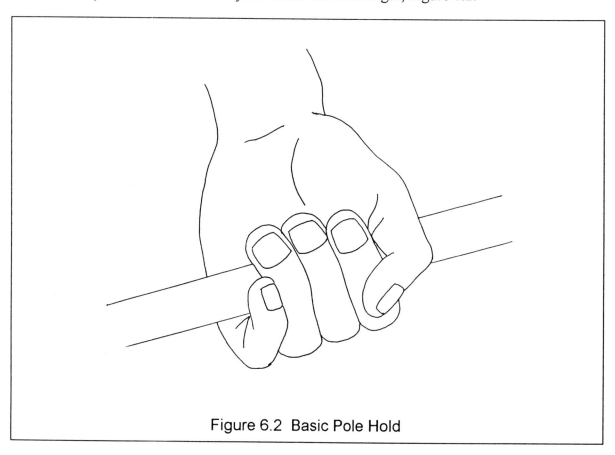

Figure 6.2 Basic Pole Hold

The reel does not involve manipulating the pole between the fingers. Rather, a flexible wrist alone does all the work to direct the course of the pole.

Make several outward full-arm swings before bending the elbow and trying a shoulder circle behind the same side that holds the pole. Figure 6.3 opposite.

From a slow start, build up momentum and stretch out the shoulders with the full-arm circle. A loose ring grip on the centre of the pole will allow the shoulder circle to flow. Keep concentrating on what you are doing in order to avoid hitting yourself.

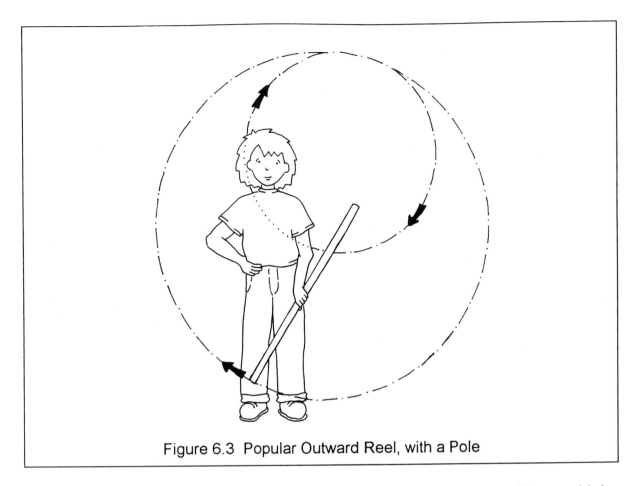

Figure 6.3 Popular Outward Reel, with a Pole

The reel has a mesmerizing effect, particularly with fire equipment. It is possible to twirl the pole between the fingers in the shoulder circle, although the move arguably looks better done fast and with the wrist alone. Try the inward direction of full-arm and shoulder circles next.

Inward reel with a pole.

The inward direction is traditionally used in Peking Opera-style spear manipulation and the secret is to let your wrist flex into the shoulder circle, rather than trying to turn your elbow.

There are many club swinging moves that can be tailored for use with other props. Certain pole moves are illustrated in this guide and many of these movements will work with either one or two poles. However, rings and flags can also be made to spin in very attractive swinging arcs. Those readers interested in practical circus skills will be able adapt the flowing movements developed by club swinging for use with a whole range of equipment from ribbons, rings, flags, balls and devil sticks, even hats and umbrellas!

Explore the integration of swinging into other performance arts, particularly dance, to gain the full benefit of your improved coordination and fitness.

Lesson 7
Hand Circles with the Ball-and-Socket Grip

This lesson introduces two hand circles which are the twin moves to those previously taught in Lesson 4. Upper-front and lower-back circles are made on the vertical plane and use the ball-and-socket grip.

Ball-and-Socket Grip

The knob of the club is the *ball* and the hand makes a *socket* with thumb and first two fingers. Figure 7.1.

The joint formed is reliable, and yet the club should be able to swing freely as it rolls around within the grasp.

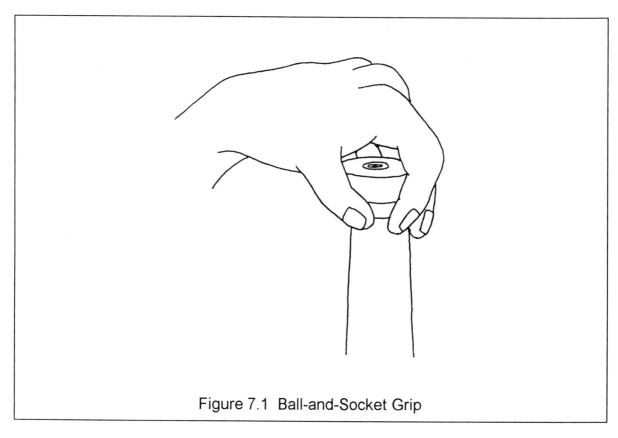

Figure 7.1 Ball-and-Socket Grip

Upper-Front Hand Circles

The upper-front position is made high and with the hands held above each shoulder. These circles are twins of shoulder circles (Lesson 4, page 19), but at the front of the body instead of the back. Use the ball-and-socket grip to rotate the club.

First swing a single outward, upper-front hand circle.
Both hands, synchronous, outward, upper-front hand circles.
Alternating time, outward, upper-front hand circles.

Bend your elbow with these tricks and the plane to aim for is the vertical or wall plane straight in front of the body. Keep the clubs a little apart so that they do not collide.

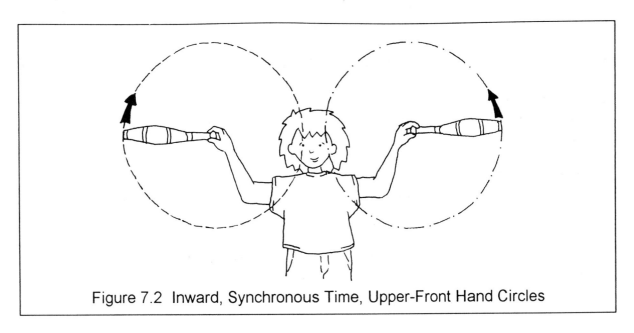

Figure 7.2 Inward, Synchronous Time, Upper-Front Hand Circles

Inward direction, synchronous, upper-front hand circles - Figure 7.2.
Inward, alternating time, upper-front hand circles.
Parallel left and right, upper-front hand circles.

Upper-front hand circles are fairly tiring to practise since the clubs are held up high. A surprisingly large amount of energy must be expended to keep lifting the weight of the arms and the clubs. If you begin to feel cramp, make a couple of club swings with the more restful full-arm circle, or just shake out your arms.

The upper-front circle can also be made with the arms held out straight to the sides - see Figure 7.3.

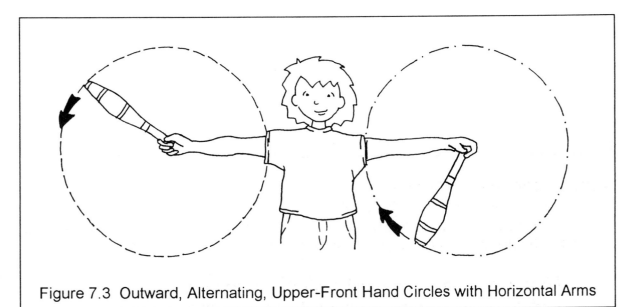

Figure 7.3 Outward, Alternating, Upper-Front Hand Circles with Horizontal Arms

Lower-Back Hand Circles
Lower-back circles are twinned with lower-front circles (Lesson 4) in that they are performed low, at hip level. However, these circles are made at the back of the body and you must use the ball-and-socket grip instead of the ring grip.

Swing a single outward, lower-back hand circle - Figure 7.4.
Try swinging outward, lower-back circles with both hands in synch.

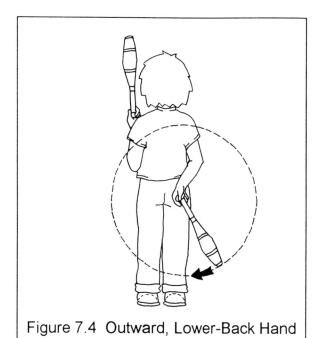

Figure 7.4 Outward, Lower-Back Hand Circle (right hand viewed from behind)

Then, synchronous time, lower-back circles made inwards.
Parallel left and right lower-back circles.

Continuous circles performed behind the body are not easy. I expect that you will find the clubs knock together at first, so take the above exercises at a slow pace. Do not spend long on these if you are having difficulties. This is because changing between front and back circles is a more natural swing than continuous rotations behind the body.

Upper-Front and Shoulder Circles

Combinations of upper-front and shoulder circles (upper-backs) are pretty and, for many people, easier than any of the continuous ball-and-socket grip moves. The clubs swing in turn, first to the front and then behind the body. If the clubs are correctly held between the thumb and first finger, you will be able to learn a smooth change in grip from a ball-and-socket grip at the front, to a ring grip behind the shoulder.

Begin with just one hand swinging outward direction alternating upper-front and shoulder circles. Next make synchronous, upper-front and shoulder circles first outward and then inward. Figure 7.5 shows a plan view of the outward movements.

There is a pleasant flow when combining front and back moves. The club should trace a figure 8 pattern with the cross-over occurring directly above your shoulder. This is shown in a view from above in Figure 7.5.

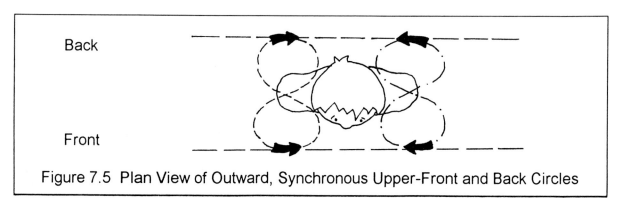

Back

Front

Figure 7.5 Plan View of Outward, Synchronous Upper-Front and Back Circles

Alternating time (short reel done up high), outward and then inward upper-front and shoulder circles. Lastly, swing the combination in parallel time, left and right.

Add variety to these high position hand circles by integrating full-arm circles or, for instance, by doubling up the timing and doing two of each circle before changing. Notice also that upper-front and shoulder circles can also be made with the clubs held out to the sides at arms length. Go back to Figure 7.2 (page 29) and add an upper-back hand circle as well as a front hand circle - although this is a tiring move to keep consistently high.

Lower-Front and Back Hand Circles

This movement is more relaxing than the upper-front and shoulder circle pattern because the arms are allowed to swing low.

One hand only, try combining outward lower-front and back circles.
Synchronous time, outward, lower-front and back circles.
Alternating time, outward, lower-front and back circles (a 'low reel').

It is important to twist your wrist inward, **keeping the back of the hand against your hips** when changing between front and back positions. This inward twist of the wrist from the lower-front moving into lower-back circles is shown in Figure 7.6.

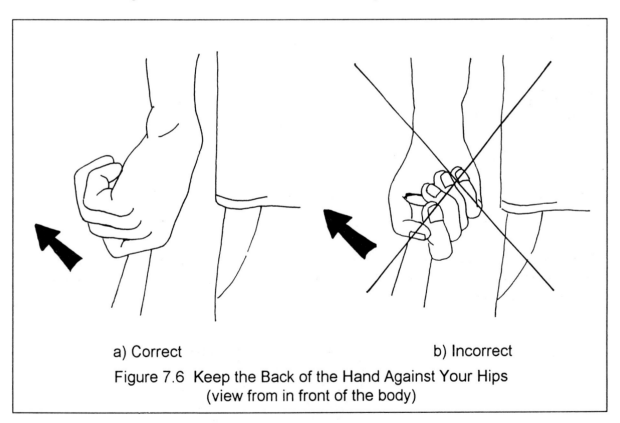

a) Correct   b) Incorrect

Figure 7.6 Keep the Back of the Hand Against Your Hips
(view from in front of the body)

Alternating lower-front and back circles is a fairly well known move called a 'low reel.' Start with just the weaker hand and introduce the stronger hand in the off beat. Once the rhythm is learnt, it is possible to swing this pattern at high speed and it is a useful trick with which to alter your timings (see Lesson 8 for tips on smooth transitions). Lower-front and back circles can also be performed with a short to medium length pole.

Reverse the low pattern's direction by swinging the lower-front circle inward. When a momentum is gained, try inward, lower-front and back circles in synchronous and then alternating time.
Parallel lower-front and back circles first left and then to the right.

Experiment with your club swinging by adding combinations of full-arm circles and upper-front or shoulder circles to the stable lower-front and back swinging pattern.

Throwing a Club From a Low Reel Swinging Pattern
Try gently throwing a single club on its swing up and outwards from a lower-front circle.

Begin a low reel, i.e., alternating lower-front and back circles. Give a gentle lift as you let go of a club at the release point near your navel on the rise of the circle. The club will spin once. Catch it with the same hand, on the outside of the pattern. Reach for the club handle as near to the knob as possible. Let the club slide down into the ring grip made by the thumb and first finger.

The throw is released from the inside of the pattern and caught again on the outside of the pattern. It is likely that the flight of the club will be slow in comparison with the swing made with the other hand. Re-adjust back into the rhythm of alternating low reels before repeating the throw and then trying the trick using your other hand. **Good**.

Lesson 8
Smooth Transitions

Effective club swinging routines have an entrancing flow, while at the same time weaving unexpected patterns. To achieve these, you must learn some techniques to change timing at will, with finesse! This lesson presents ideas on how to attain seamless transitions between tricks. The basic principle involves isolating one hand (usually one's stronger hand) and directing it to make the adjustment, while the other continues swinging.

Add a Solitary Hand Circle

In order to move from full-arm circles together into an alternating time pattern, first swing slow and even, synchronous time outward full-arm circles. Choose a single hand, either right or left, and consciously use it to make a solitary outward upper-front circle before going back to full-arm circles, now in alternating time.

Begin swinging synchronous, outward, full-arm circles. Your chosen hand does one outward, upper-front hand circle. Meanwhile, the other hand continues with full-arm circles, so that the timing changes from synchronous to alternating time - Figure 8.1. Change back.

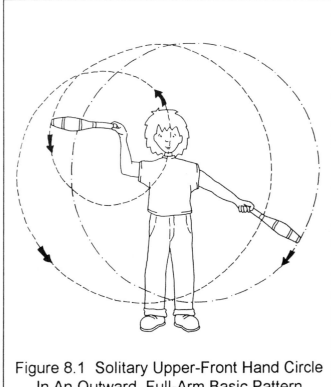

Figure 8.1 Solitary Upper-Front Hand Circle In An Outward, Full-Arm Basic Pattern

You may have to try this pattern several times since it involves a fair amount of control to isolate the two sides of the body, even for just one small hand circle! The hand that is not making the adjustment should never alter in its speed or rhythm from the basic full-arm circle.

Strengthen your weaker hand by using it to change timing, instead of always making adjustments with just the dominant hand.

Variations include performing this move in the inward direction, or with a single lower-back circle. Try inward, full-arm circles with a lower-front hand circle to change rhythm.

There do appear to be combinations of patterns and adjustments that force collisions. The message from this is to be careful to try any new adjustment moves slowly at first.

Double Up One Hand Circle

Start from a figure 8 pattern of lower-front and back circles (the low reel) in alternating time. Concentrate on one hand and mentally instruct it to double up the front circle.

Swing a low reel. The strong hand only performs a double front hand circle to change to synchronous time, outward, lower-front and backs. Change back into alternating time by doubling just the strong hand's front circle again. Repeat.

This method allows a very smooth change of pattern without stopping. Variations include the same change inward and also in a high alternating upper-front and back circle pattern. Try the extra lower-front circle with your weaker hand as an exercise to develop that wrist.

Isolation of Each Side with Split-Level Swinging

It can be attractive to swing a high pattern set against a contrasting low pattern on the other side of the body. The transition is via half a full-arm circle. In either the outward or the inward direction try the following pattern.

From alternating, lower-front and back circles, one hand rises to begin high and alternating upper-front and shoulder circles. Figure 8.2. Swap levels apart again on the opposite side.

The diagram only shows a single circle at each level because front and back circles are overlapping from the front view. Some variations include split-level swinging with continuous front or back hand circles, either in synchronous or alternating time.

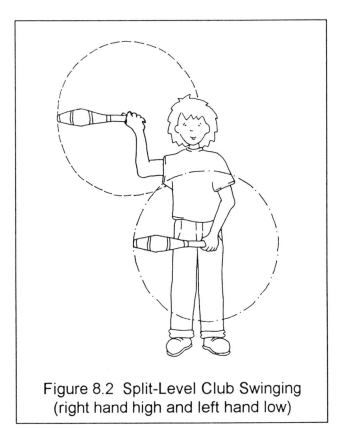

Figure 8.2 Split-Level Club Swinging
(right hand high and left hand low)

Changing Direction by Raising One Knee

When performing lower-front circles, it is possible to stop a club briefly by raising your knee. An example is to start swinging lower-front and back circles in alternating time (the low reel). On the outside of the outward lower-front swing, lift one leg and allow the same hand's club to stop horizontally across your knee for a second. Change direction with that club and begin swinging a parallel pattern.

Try this change with both hands, each knee and with a combination of timings, including patterns that incorporate full-arm circles.

34

One Hand Does a Free Style Solo

From a swinging pattern that you find relaxing, just one hand can leave the other to perform a completely different move, or set of moves. This is what I call a free style. Such moves are fun, but require complete concentration, both to leave the symmetrical pattern and to rejoin it again at exactly the right moment. The next exercise starts from a low reel and once you have mastered it, try it while smiling!

Swing fast, alternating, outward, lower-front and back circles. One hand leaves the pattern to perform a greatly slowed-down full-arm circle, perhaps with an upper-front circle. It can rejoin the original move either in synchronous time or off-synch.

Attempt to make solos with each hand and at various tempos. For instance, the free style could be at twice the speed of the basic pattern. Use your imagination to think of impressive and original free style movements.

Lesson 9
Horizontal Plane Hand Circles

The horizontal plane is flat and parallel to the floor. This dimension is not as frequently used as the vertical planes in club swinging and this may be because it is difficult for an audience ever to see a fully rounded pattern. Nevertheless, the extra plane in your vocabulary of moves will add interest to routines and give you greater flexibility. The horizontal planes to aim for are high - under or over shoulder level as shown in Figure 9.1.

Horizontal planes are often used in pole and baton manipulation. This lesson contains some stick twirls and I suggest that you try them with a relatively short pole, such as a devil stick, so that it can swing underneath your arms.

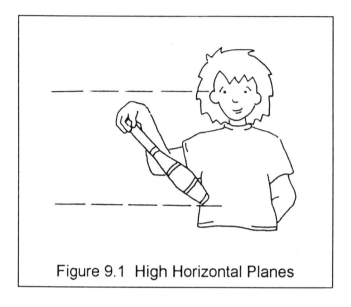

Figure 9.1 High Horizontal Planes

Under-Arm Hand Circles

The club is held in the ball-and-socket grip (Lesson 7, page 28). Outward circles are made when clubs move from the mid line of the body outward to the front and then circle back toward the body on the sides. Inward circles are the exact opposite, i.e., movements are reversed.

With the club facing downward at the front, rotate a single club in the horizontal plane underneath the arm, outward - Figure 9.2. Change direction and then swap hands. Synchronous time under-arm hand circles with both hands, in both directions.

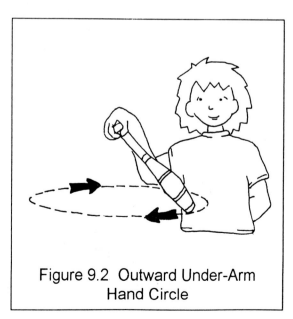

Figure 9.2 Outward Under-Arm Hand Circle

Keep your arms slightly apart so that the clubs cannot collide. Check that the clubs are as close to your arms as possible and stay horizontal. Pirouettes are easily performed with under-arm hand circles since the clubs never restrict the movement of your legs.

Alternating time outward, then inward under-arm hand circles. Finally, swing parallel left and right under-arm hand circles.

36

Over-Arm Hand Circles

This is the complement to the last move. The differences are that circles are made over-arm and use the ring grip (Lesson 3, page 15) instead of the ball-and-socket grip.

Rotate a single club horizontally above the arm. Change direction and then swap hands.
Swing synchronised outward, then inward over-arm circles. Figure 9.3. Also try over-arm circles in the alternating and parallel timings.

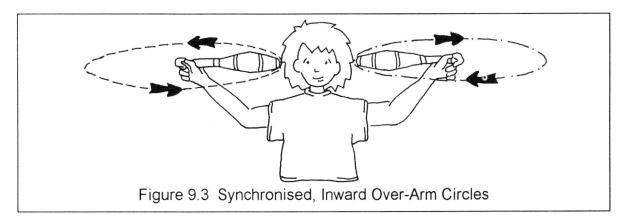

Figure 9.3 Synchronised, Inward Over-Arm Circles

I find over-arm circles more testing than circles swung under-arm. The wrist has to make a quick flicking motion to give the circle its impetus. It's a bit like swinging an old-fashioned football rattle. Be careful to distance the clubs from possibly hitting your chin by keeping your arms outstretched. Do not spend long perfecting over-arm circles as the next trick incorporating both over-and under-arm circles is easier than continuous over-arm movements.

Over and Under-Arm Circles (Figure 8's Horizontally)

Figure 8 movements seem more natural club swings than performing repeated circles either over or under-arm. You will mainly use the ball-and-socket grip, with the club momentarily entering the ring grip for the over-arm spin.

With one hand, begin swinging repeated under-arm circles. Flick your wrist over to make an over-arm circle and then continue making figure 8's. Synchronised over and under-arm hand circles both in the outward and inward directions - Figure 9.4. Alternating time over- and under-arm circles in both directions, then parallel left and right.

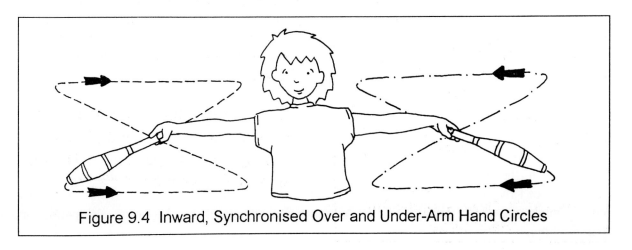

Figure 9.4 Inward, Synchronised Over and Under-Arm Hand Circles

Different positions for these over and under-arm moves include holding the arms out directly in front of the swinger or with the arms stretched to the sides. You are likely to find horizontal hand circles tiring as the arms and clubs must be raised up.

It is possible to move around your space in very attractive pirouettes while swinging circles on the flat plane. Try turning with horizontal full-arm circles in the same direction as your parallel left or right over and under-arm circles.

Follow time is explained in Lesson 11 using a forward cross-follow. A follow time pattern can also be swung on the horizontal plane. It is established by starting a figure 8 pattern in parallel time and speeding up with one hand until it is half a circle in front. Once you have learnt the vertical cross-follow (pages 42-43), try the move on the horizontal plane at first allowing the over-arm circles to rise above your head. Later, decrease the size of the pattern to just flat circles directly over and under your arms, which are held outstretched and stationary. This horizontal cross-follow can be done in two directions, either with the left or the right hand leading.

Over and Under-Arm Helicopters with a Short Pole

Use a medium to short pole such as a baton or devil stick. It must not be longer than twice the length of your arm, or else it will not pass under-arm.

Hold the pole's centre between thumb and first finger in a light pinch. Decide on one end X and rotate this end in a helicopter motion so that it traces out a flat circle, parallel to the floor, over-arm. The opposite end will be doing the same, except under-arm. Figure 9.5.

A flat circle is accomplished with a rolling, circular wrist action. The elbow bends slightly and then straightens as though making an exaggerated stirring motion. Keep the arm high and the body straight.

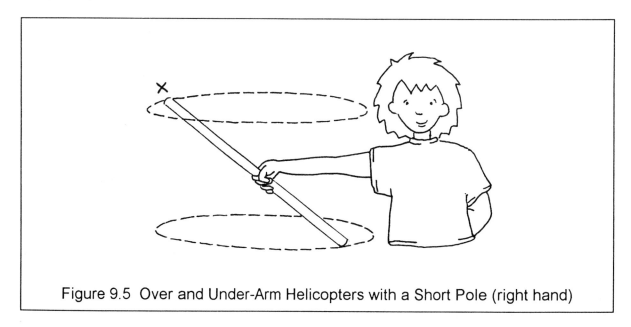

Figure 9.5 Over and Under-Arm Helicopters with a Short Pole (right hand)

Flat spins on the horizontal plane can be used to build up speed for additionally twirling the stick between the fingers when over-arm. The basic flat helicopter move can be done with either hand, outwards, inwards and with two poles in any of synchronous, alternating or parallel time.

Lesson 10
Forward and Backward Hand Circles for Limber Wrists

Lesson 3 concentrated on forward and backward hand circles. This lesson develops the wrist action in the forward vertical plane, building up the flexibility to learn the popular cross-follow.

Hand Circles Inside the Arms
During this movement the clubs swing in the gap between your arms. It makes sense to keep your arms at least shoulder width apart and always out straight. This is to allow the pattern sufficient space so that the clubs do not touch. Clubs are held in the ball-and-socket grip (Lesson 7, page 28).

With a single club, make forward circles on the inside of the arm - Figures 10.1 and 10.2. Swap hands.
Both hands, synchronous forward hand circles inside the arms.

Forward movements are made by starting with the clubs straight out in front. Drop the clubs away, then bring them back towards the body as they rise. Inside-arm patterns are much more difficult than outside-arm patterns because the clubs are swinging in the restricted space between your arms and are likely to collide. Go slowly and work on keeping the spins as near to your arms as possible.

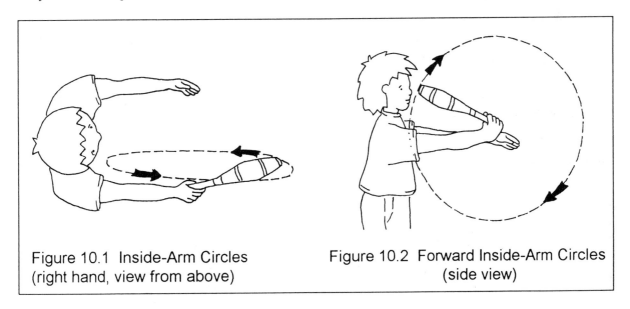

Figure 10.1 Inside-Arm Circles
(right hand, view from above)

Figure 10.2 Forward Inside-Arm Circles
(side view)

Follow the above sequence of moves, now in the backward direction.

The backward pattern is similar to the motion of beckoning someone.

Spend only a short amount of time practising inside-arm circles and progress next to the somewhat more natural figure 8 pattern.

Figure 8 Inside and Outside Hand Circles
This move can be done very fast and is worth learning both with clubs and with a pole. The ends of the clubs draw out a figure 8. It is much easier to swap between inside and outside hand circles than to form repeated circles between the arms.

A single hand swings alternating inside then outside forward hand circles with the wrist sweeping a forward figure 8 pattern. Swap hands and repeat. Next try synchronous, forward inside and outside hand circles. Lastly swing parallel figure 8's, Figure 10.3 (plan view).

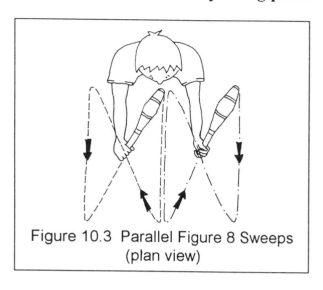

Figure 10.3 Parallel Figure 8 Sweeps (plan view)

Your elbow bends, with a flexible wrist principally turning the swinging motion. The clubs continually change between the two sides of your arm. Keep circles flat to the vertical plane and adjust so that the clubs trace full circles when seen from the side.

Figure 8 Sweeps With a Pole

Use a broom stick to learn this satisfying pattern. The pole in the figure has a spearhead which is simply used to distinguish the end with the path trail. Hold the centre of your pole in the notch between your thumb and forefinger (Figure 6.2, page 26).

Sweep the pole forward so that the ends alternate inside and outside the arm in a figure 8. Figure 10.4.

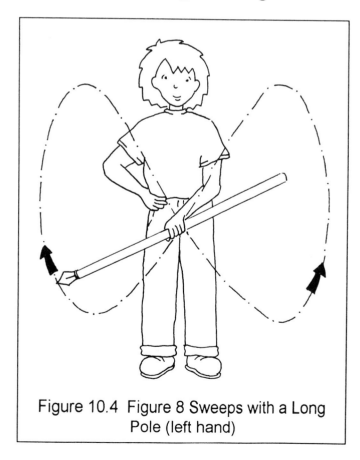

Figure 10.4 Figure 8 Sweeps with a Long Pole (left hand)

With practice, the pattern can be made at very high speed and is then an impressive trick. Mind your head when using a long pole and stand side on to the audience for full effect.

(Jugglers - this move is equivalent to a club flourish, with the club held between the thumb and first finger for the whole move).

Backward Figure 8's

The opposite of the previous trick is to make figure 8 sweeps with the wrist turning backward. First mime the motion with each wrist. Start by holding the clubs with a ring grip (Figure 3.2, page 15). You may choose to change into ball-and-socket grip for inside-arm hand circles if this grip feels more comfortable.

A single hand swings alternating inside and outside hand circles sweeping backward. Swap hands and repeat. With both hands, try synchronous figure 8 sweeps inside and outside the arm. Next, parallel backward figure 8 sweeps.

As well as practising backward figure 8 swings with clubs, try the same backward motion with a single pole.

Cross-Overs

This is a type of movement in which the wrists are crossed in front of the body. Choose to have either the left or right hand on top.

Begin from a basic pattern of synchronous forward hand circles outside the arms. Add cross-over swings where your hands cross to perform the inside hand circle of a figure 8 swing.

Figure 8 moves are very attractive and are also building blocks to what is, perhaps, the single most popular move in club swinging - the cross-follow, as taught the next lesson.

Exercise Routine

From starting position (Figure 1.4, page 8), try the following short routine with each movement repeated 8 times.

1 Synchronous forward hand circles outside the arms down to touch the ground (page 16).
2 Synchronous backward hand circles outside the arms reaching up high (page 16).
3 Synchronous forward cross-overs in combination with forward hand circles outside.
4 Synchronous backward cross-overs in combination with backward hand circles outside.
5 Alternating time, backward full-arm circles (page 13).
6 Half pirouette into forward, alternating full-arm circles (page 14).
   Stop with both hands held high.

These moves are repeated in Section B of the Mass Fire Routine (pages 83 - 85).

Lesson 11
Follow Time and the Cross-Follow

This lesson introduces some of the most exquisite movements in club swinging. Follow time patterns occur when one club exactly follows the path of the other by half a circle. Both clubs describe precisely the same figure 8, which effectively doubles up the visual force of the movement. Many follow time patterns look as if your wrists are hooked together with the clubs always level, as though they were attached like one straight pole.

Follow Time: Usually with a class of figure 8 pattern, one club leads and the other follows so that the clubs stay half a circle apart at all times.

Forward Cross-Follow with Full-Arm Circles, then Hand Circles

First learn the cross-follow (sometimes called the chase) with full-arm circles. Once you have the feel of the movement, it is possible to reduce the size of the pattern to the popular cross-follow around the wrists. With a club held in the solid grip, make forward full-arm figure 8 circles. These are enlarged versions of the forward figure 8 pattern in Lesson 10 (page 40).

One hand only swings forward, full-arm figure 8 sweeps. Swap hands and repeat. Still with a single hand, add asymmetry to the full-arm pattern by making each arm trace out one circle on its own side of the body and two circles on the opposite side - Figure 11.1.

The asymmetry is unusual in club swinging. Only for cross-follow patterns does each hand perform two swings on the far side of the body and one on the near side, with a total of three circles in a full cycle.

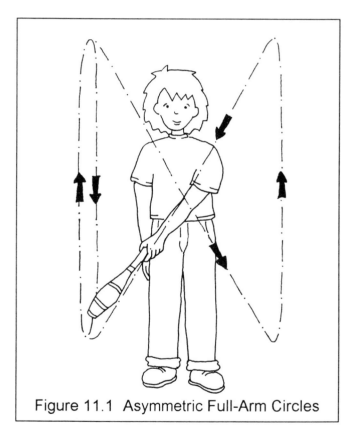

Figure 11.1 Asymmetric Full-Arm Circles

Move on to using two clubs and try to link both sides together into a continuous figure 8 cycle. There are now a total of six swings in the cycle, three on each side.

Start swinging forward full-arm circles in alternating time. Right arm swings to cross-over the left and the left arm completes a circle under the right arm before the right swings back to its own side.

Next swing the right hand over and then under the left arm. The arms uncross as the right hand returns with a figure 8 sweep to the right. Cross them again on the right side of the body with the left hand over the right. Continue crossing and uncrossing arms, changing sides each time - Figure 11.2.

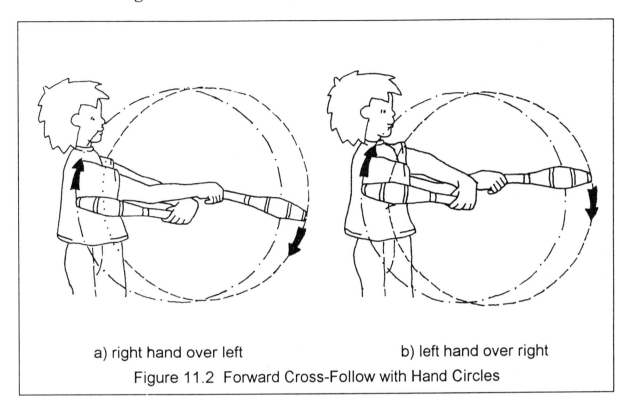

a) right hand over left   b) left hand over right

Figure 11.2 Forward Cross-Follow with Hand Circles

Both arms are taking the same path, but at a staggered rhythm, with the right hand leading by half a circle and the left following behind. The right hand chases the left hand over to the right side, then the left Hand chases the right hand to the left side. The clubs are always at 180 degrees to one another as if they were a single pole rather than two separate objects.

If your arms get into a knot, return to swinging forward full-arm circles in alternating time before attempting the trick again. Once the full-arm crossing movement begins to flow, reduce the size of your circles from those centered on your shoulders, to your elbows and finally to circles rotating around your wrist. Use a loose ring grip and aim to make the palm side of both wrists stay permanently in contact.

Try counting how many times a club passes your hip on each side. It should be three times past one side, then three times past the other. This is a difficult trick to understand. However, with several practice sessions, you will eventually master the popular swinging motion of fast circles chasing around the wrist, the forward cross-follow.

Backward Cross-Follow with Full-Arm Circles, then Hand Circles
It is possible to swing a cross-follow motion in the backward direction, although many people find the movement rather unnatural. Nevertheless, it is worth learning the pattern backwards in order to progress and eventually master the cross-follow in a full circle (the fountain) which has six individual circles making up this beautiful, if technically demanding pattern. As before, start with wide large arm-sweeps, making them slowly smaller until your wrists seem hooked together. Use a solid grip for full-arm patterns and the ring grip for hand circles.

One hand only performs backward full-arm figure 8 swings. Add asymmetry by making each arm trace out one circle on its own side of the body and two circles on the opposite side, still going backward.

With a single arm, swing the backward movements of the cross-follow, first with large circles then reducing the size to small hand circles. If the hand circles are problematic, re-attempt Lesson 10's description of backward figure 8 inside and outside hand circles (page 40). Your inside backward hand circle is initially likely to be weak. Now for the move with both hands.

Swing backward full-arm circles in alternating time. Make your right arm swing to cross-over the left and the left arm completes a circle under the right arm before swinging back to its own side. The arms have uncrossed and you should next cross them again on the right side of the body.

Continue to cross and unravel your arms using the extended figure 8 motion of the cross-follow. There must be three circles in the backward cross-follow with each hand and you could check this by counting how many times the clubs pass your hip. Always sweep the clubs backward and away from you.

Don't worry if your arms get tangled when you first attempt to make backward cross-follows. Decide where your arms should have gone in order to keep the crossing and uncrossing cycle going. If you find yourself swinging forwards instead of backwards, stop and play back the motion in reverse using wider circles. You are ultimately aiming to make a small, backward figure 8 pattern centre around the wrists in follow time.

Move around your space and also practise going from a cross-follow in either forward or backward directions into an alternating time full-arm pirouette (Lesson 2, page 14). **Fantastic!**

Lesson 12
Exploring Parallel Moves

Parallel movements are worth examining in further detail as they offer the most adaptable timing from which to make smooth transitions between tricks. Strong parallels are also the key to learning follow time patterns. However, it is quite demanding of the swinger to gain a perfect parallel time as both sides, in both directions, must be equally capable.

Before studying this lesson it will help to review the material in Lesson 7, particularly upper-front and shoulder circles (page 30) and lower-front and back hand circles (page 31).

Parallel Full-Arm and Shoulder Circle Combination

Begin swinging full-arm circles in parallel. Add shoulder (upper-back) circles. Notice that one side describes outward, full-arm and shoulder circles while the other swings inward circles. Initially choose your stronger hand to perform the direction of circles that you find most difficult, probably the inward.

From start position, swing parallel, full-arm circles left. Bend your elbow to add a shoulder circle each side of your head, in parallel - Figure 12.1. Repeat 4 cycles. Stop neatly and swing these parallel movements to the right.

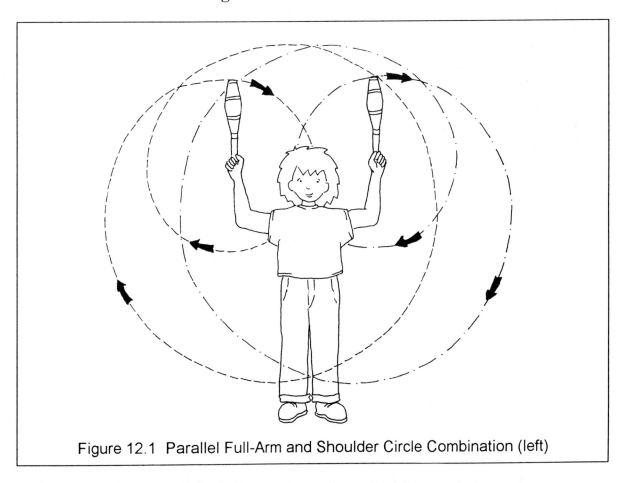

Figure 12.1 Parallel Full-Arm and Shoulder Circle Combination (left)

Remember to keep your hands shoulder-width apart. If one side is lagging behind the other, then stop and perform the move with the weaker side in isolation to help that particular wrist's motion.

The Windmill, Full-Arm and Shoulder Circles in Follow Time.

This move builds upon the previous combination of parallel full-arm and shoulder circles. In a windmill the hand circles are made directly in the centre at the top of the pattern.

Start swinging parallel full-arm circles to the left. Add shoulder circles in parallel time. Then, as soon as the shoulder circles have been completed, speed up slightly with the right hand. Let this hand progressively increase its lead until it is just half a circle ahead and you can introduce circles directly behind the head - Figure 12.2. Stop, change direction to parallels right and then move into the windmill right with the left hand leading.

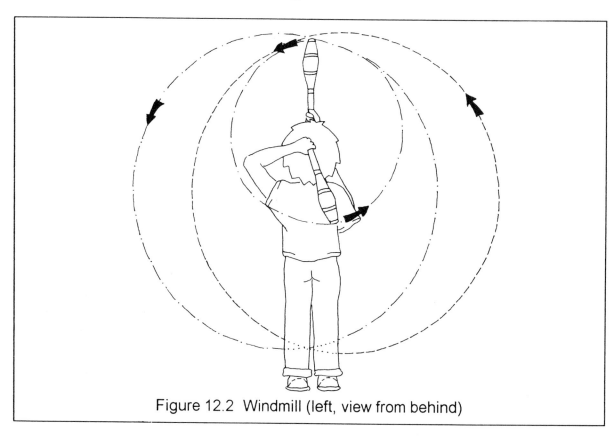

Figure 12.2 Windmill (left, view from behind)

Go slowly while learning this move, or else your clubs will bump the back of your head. Watch a mirror to check that your shoulder circles are flat to the vertical or "wall" plane. A pure windmill is performed when the upper-back position circles are directly behind the head. It is possible to extend the windmill using upper-front circles as well as upper-back (shoulder) circles in follow time. This encircling of the head is lovely to watch and very exciting with fire clubs!

Parallel Full-Arm and Lower-Back Hand Circle Combination

Here the parallel hand circles are made at hip level in the form of lower-back circles.

Swing parallel full-arm circles to the left. Still in parallel, add one lower-back circle on either side of your body at hip level. Circles will be outward with left hand and inward with the right hand. Figure 12.3. Stop and change direction.

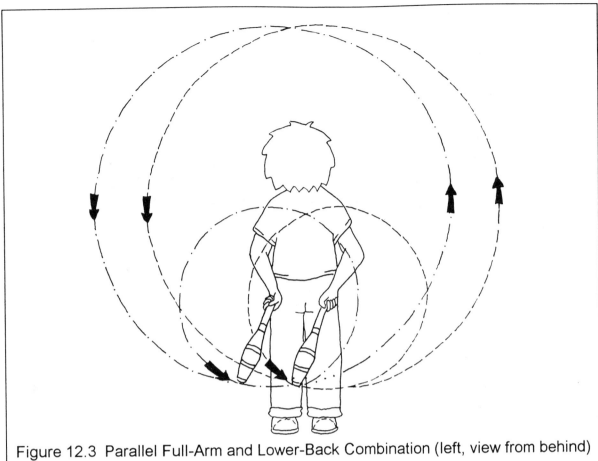

Figure 12.3 Parallel Full-Arm and Lower-Back Combination (left, view from behind)

If your lower-back hand circles are weak, then practise them individually until the movement is smoother. Look back at Lesson 7 which explains strengthening moves such as lower-front and back hand circles in parallel. During the transitions between the front and back of the body, remember to swing the wrist inward and to keep the back of your hand against your hip as shown in Figure 7.6 (page 31), rather than uncomfortably twisting the palm upwards.

Next try the more advanced combination move of both upper and lower-back circles linked by half full-arm circles.

Swinging Between the Legs

Stand with your feet more than shoulder width apart, but at a distance that is easy to balance.

Begin swinging slow, outward full-arm circles with your right hand. Then, passing your mid line and coming in from the right side, flex your wrist to loop back a single lower-back circle between your legs and out on the left side at the front. Continue the full-arm circle upwards. Figure 12.4, following page.

The swing between the legs makes a small loop back on itself at the bottom of a full-arm circle. It helps to keep your knees straight.

Repeat the looped swing several times and swap hands and direction. Then try parallel movements with one or both clubs swinging between your legs.

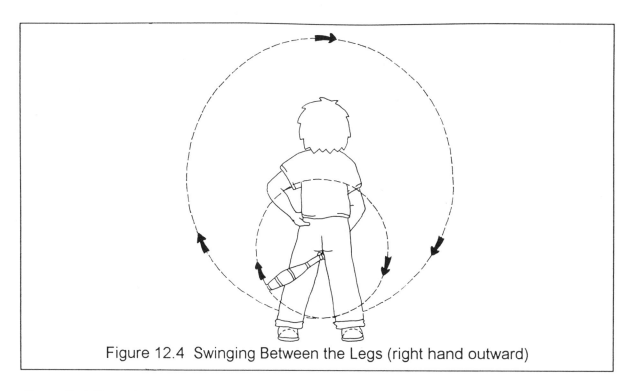

Figure 12.4 Swinging Between the Legs (right hand outward)

Parallel Pendulums

A pendulum swing does not complete a full circle rotation. Instead, there is half a swing from side to side, like the motion of a see-saw or pendulum. Twist your body for these movements.

Facing sideways, swing downward into parallel lower-back circles either side of your hips and up on the other side of your body. Stop at shoulder level - Figure 12.5. Change to swing forward arm circles down again and repeat the move, twisting with the half turn.

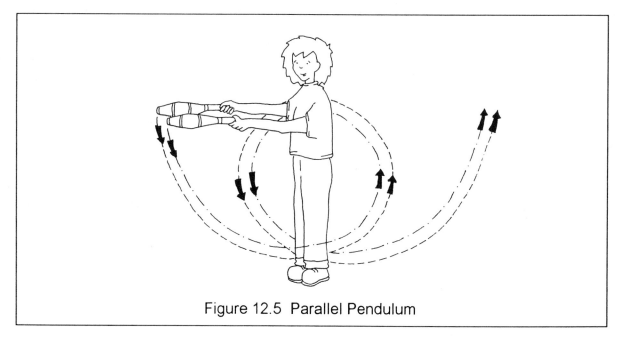

Figure 12.5 Parallel Pendulum

This class of pendulum can also be done up high, with shoulder circles inserted in the place of lower-back circles. The pendulum is a very useful move for turning around, but will look controlled only if you use precise stops. The clubs can be thrown from a rising pendulum swing where both clubs are released together and spun to the same height.

Lesson 13
Snake Curls

Snakes are a category of club swinging move in which the clubs wrap around the arm like two coiled serpents. They are intriguing to watch! There is less swing in these moves than the more usual wide circles and, therefore, hardly any momentum to carry the club around. This makes learning snakes challenging, but they are satisfying and will add a mark of class to your club swinging repertoire. The arms will have to work quite hard, so use lightweight clubs and be sure to flex the wrist and shoulders thoroughly before you start.

Snake Grip

With the knob upward, grasp the club's neck and put the ball of your hand against the handle. Place your forefinger over the knob to steady the grip. Figure 13.1.

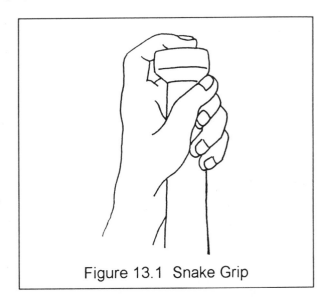

Figure 13.1 Snake Grip

A snake grip is very different from other club swinging holds because your hand attaches to the upturned club handle rather than around the knob. During a snake, the club is forced to stay close to the forearm instead of having an independent swing. The elbow is the centre point of the pattern.

Although the most popular snake is an outward (or regular) shoulder snake, I have decided to introduce this category of movements with a somewhat easier pattern called a snake curl. This trick is essentially flat and resembles the horizontal patterns of Lesson 9. A useful stationary point in which to gain concentration before attempting a snake is the cradle.

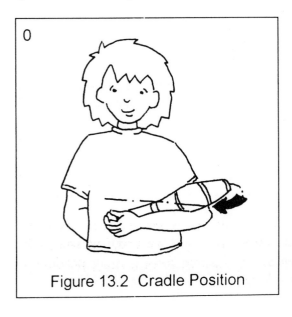

Figure 13.2 Cradle Position

Cradle Position

Hold a club in the snake grip and rest it on your forearm with your elbow bent as though you were cradling an infant. Figure 13.2.

The cradle is a restful position as your arm supports the weight of the club. Cradles are used as the starting position for the spiraling tricks on the horizontal (flat) plane taught in this lesson.

Inward Snake Curls

A curl pattern is a figure 8 performed underneath and over the top of the arms, very much like the over and under-arm hand circles of Lesson 9 (page 37). Hold only one club with a snake grip and cradle the club, resting it on your inside forearm. There are two circles in total and figures are labelled with the turns starting with the cradle 0, ½ up to 2 circles.

Curl your wrist inward until the body of the club passes close under the arm. Then bend the elbow and flick the wrist upward to direct the club's swivel over-arm and back to the cradle. Figure 13.3.

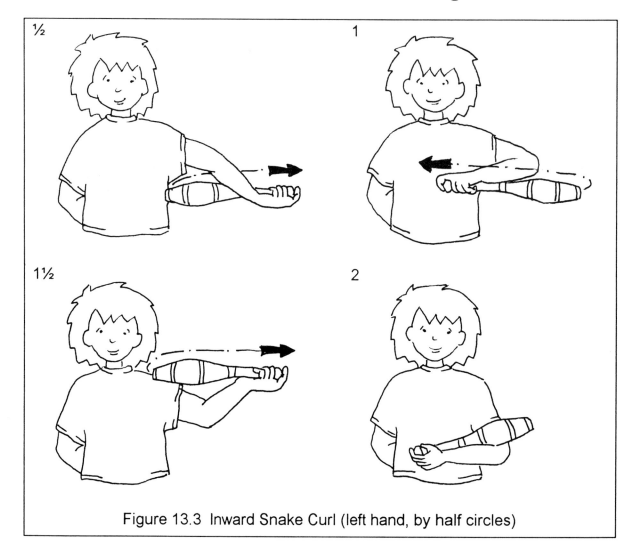

Figure 13.3 Inward Snake Curl (left hand, by half circles)

For an inward snake curl, first trace a circle under the arm with the club in a snake grip. The second part is a flat snake circle over the arm. Don't worry if this spiral movement feels weird at first. The club stays in the horizontal plane, flat and parallel with the floor and remains next to the forearm.

Synchronous time inward snake curls.
Alternating time inward snake curls.

Learn the pattern in alternating time by making continuous snake curl with your weaker hand and then introduce your stronger side on the off-beat.

Outward Snake Curls

This pattern is the same figure 8 curl pattern, but in the opposite direction to the previous move. Try the previous figures in backwards order. Start from a cradle with one hand.

Open your arm to allow the club to travel forward and outward, performing an over-arm circle until the club is resting behind the forearm. Then turn the wrist down and outward so that the club moves under-arm and back in to a cradle. Swap hands.

In the first half of the move the arm stretches out straight, allowing the club to slip over to the back of the forearm. Then, once the club is behind the arm, curl your wrist under and bend your elbow to direct the club back underneath the arm. Try these patterns with two clubs.

Synchronous time outward snake curls.
Alternating time outward snake curls.
Parallel left and right.

Parallel snake curls are very tricky movements. One club rotates in the inward direction and the other outwards. In order to start parallels, one hand must be half way through its figure 8 when the other side begins with a normal cradle. The two clubs should have their bases pointing in the same direction, flat and in parallel, throughout this movement.

Lesson 14
Regular Snakes

The most popular snake in club swinging is performed at shoulder level on the vertical or 'wall' plane and seen from the front. Your elbows should be the stationary centre points around which the clubs rotate. The clubs coil around the wrists, incorporating two full circles and a 'throw-off,' making three circles in all. The turns are labelled by quarters from 0, ¼ all the way up to 3.

Outward Full Snake

Hold an upturned club in a snake grip (Figure 13.1, page 49), forefinger over the club knob. Figure 14.1 shows the starting position. Watch that your elbow is at the height of your shoulder and that the body of the club is resting behind your upper arm. The palm of the hand should face outward (away from your face) to begin a regular shoulder snake.

Figure 14.1 Starting Position, Outward Snake

First Circle - Start the club in an arc outward, away from your head. The base of the club is brought upward as the wrist turns down and in towards your chest. Continue the small circle until the club passes underneath the forearm, then turn the wrist to face outward again.

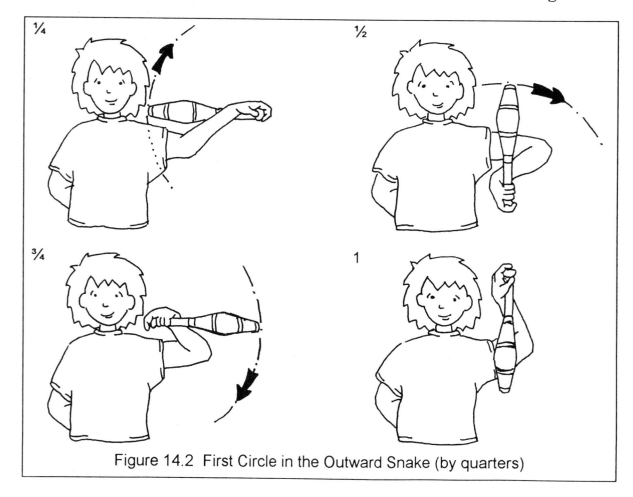

Figure 14.2 First Circle in the Outward Snake (by quarters)

Notice that at the end of the first circle you are in a position similar to the original starting position (Figure 14.1), except that the club is **now in front of the arm**. Crucially, you must turn your wrist to face outward before beginning the second circle.

Second Circle - Start position shown in the last picture of Figure 14.2. Push the club outward and downward, slowly circling in front of the arm. The club moves into the cradle position after three quarters of a circle before resting vertically behind your upper arm. Figure 14.3.

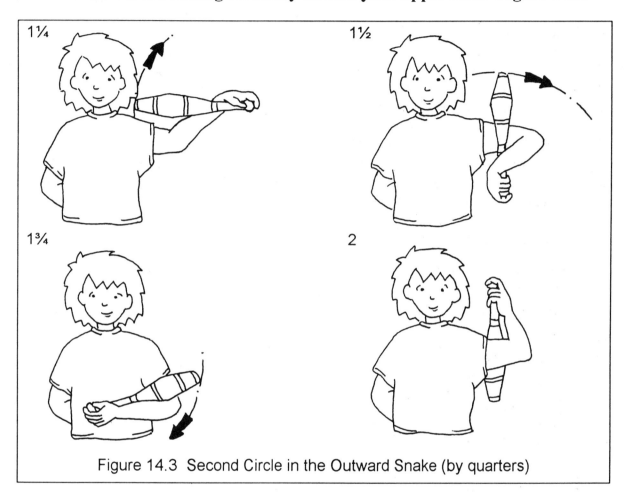

Figure 14.3 Second Circle in the Outward Snake (by quarters)

Throw-Off

A throw-off completes the outward snake by turning the wrist from facing inward (towards the head) to an outward angle and ready to restart the snake movement. During a throw-off the club swings a full circle behind the shoulder.

Begin with a snake grip facing inward and the club behind your shoulder. Release all your fingers except your forefinger and thumb from the neck of the club. Use a sharp flick of the wrist to spin the club once outward - Figure 14.4 on the following page. Regain a snake grip in the start position.

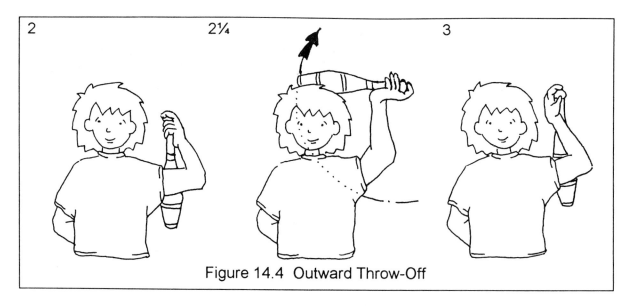

Figure 14.4 Outward Throw-Off

An interesting variation on the straight throw-off shown in Figure 14.4 is to direct a vertical club around the back of your head.

The regular shoulder snake is mastered when you can link smooth cycles consisting of first circles, second circles and a throw-off. With a club in each hand try to make:

Synchronous time outward snakes.
Alternating time outward snakes.

Well done! Snakes work the wrist and arm fairly hard and so it will be an effort to keep the clubs held high and exactly on the vertical wall plane. Either swing some full-arm and hand circle patterns or else take a rest before learning the following half snake movements.

Outward Half Snakes
First or second-half snakes can be performed without the other circle by making slight adjustments to the regular snake. The snake is thereby shortened to two circles instead of three.

First-Half Outward Snake
To complete just a first-half snake, start as for a regular snake with the club behind the shoulder and make an early throw-off. This throw-off is after the first circle when the arm is in the position in Figure 14.5. Importantly, your hand still faces the head just before the throw-off instead of turning outward as in Figure 14.2,(1). The early throw-off returns the club to a normal start position (Figure 14.1).

Figure 14.5 Early Throw-Off Point

Second-Half Outward Snakes

Begin later in the snake with the club resting in front of the arm, as shown in Figure 14.2,(1). Complete the second-half snake (Figure 14.3). The throw-off is slightly different from normal because you aim to end with the club in front, rather than behind, the shoulder.

Figure 14.6 Throw-Off for Continuous Second-Half Outward Snakes

Transition From Full-Arm and Shoulder Circles Into a Snake Grip

From an outward full-arm circle, bend the elbow as the club comes past the head, allowing the club to swing down into a shoulder circle. Catch the club in a snake grip during the outer half of the shoulder circle as the club is lowered from its peak. Keep the momentum going and straight away begin an outward regular snake. Throw-off into a full-arm circle and repeat.

The transition from an outward shoulder circle into a regular snake can be very smooth as these circles are of similar sizes. Try linking various moves to form interesting snake combinations mixed with the classic wide arm swings in both synchronous and alternating timings.

Lesson 15
Hip Snakes

Hip snakes are low snake patterns performed with the arms down by your sides. The swinger twists the club around the hip and forearm at waist level. As with the regular shoulder snake there are two complete circles and a throw off, making three circles in the whole movement. My diagrams are of the left hand, with views from both in front and behind the body and are labelled according to the number of half circles completed from 0, ½ up to 3.

Outward Hip Snake

I first explain how to change from a ball-and-socket grip into the snake grip. Begin swinging a club in an outward, lower-back hand circle (Figure 7.4, page 30).

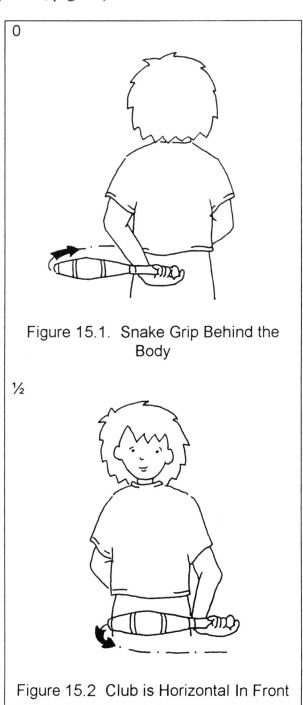

0

When the club base approaches the top of its arc, catch the handle into a snake grip with the hand behind your hip. Figure 15.1.

Figure 15.1. Snake Grip Behind the Body

½

Allow the club head to twist the wrist round to the front of the body with the club ending flat (horizontal) to the floor. Figure 15.2.

Figure 15.2 Club is Horizontal In Front

Middle Hip Snake Circle

Start from the position shown in Figure 15.2. This circle is made in front of the body.

Keeping the club flat to the ground, twist your wrist in and towards your hip to move the club head outwards in a horizontal circle. Figure 15.3, by half circles.

Notice that in Figure 15.3,1½ below the hand is pulled slightly away from the hip to allow the club space to slip under-arm.

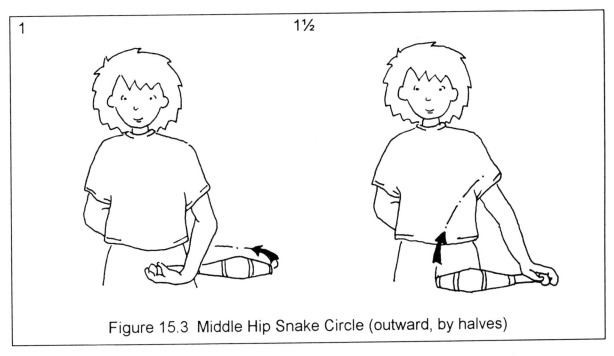

Figure 15.3 Middle Hip Snake Circle (outward, by halves)

Next, allow the club to return to the front horizontal plane by moving the club up and into a low cradle position. Figure 15.4.

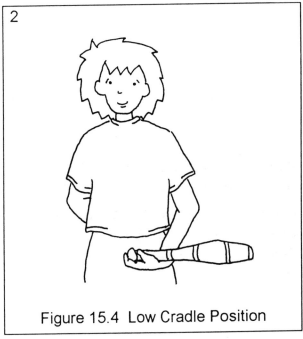

Figure 15.4 Low Cradle Position

Throw-Off

From a low cradle position, release all but your thumb and forefinger from the neck of the club to throw-off a full circle which is swung behind the body. The club ends behind the hip and you are then ready to restart a hip snake. Figure 15.5.

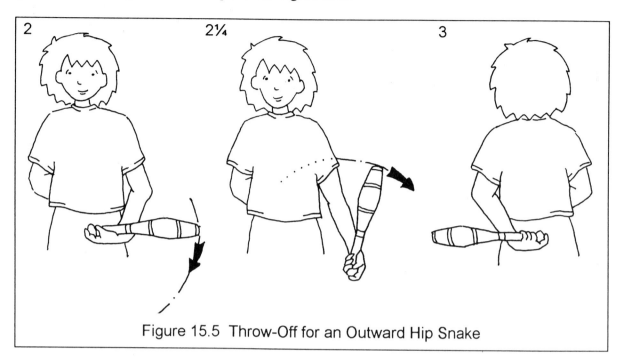

Figure 15.5 Throw-Off for an Outward Hip Snake

Continuous outward hip snakes can be performed in synchronous or alternating time.

Travelling Body Snakes

Experiment with linking hip snakes and the regular snakes of Lesson 14 (page 52) into what are called 'travelling body snakes' or 'rope snakes.' These tricks twist the clubs up and down the torso. Begin with just one hand swinging continuous outward hip snakes.

Upward - From a low cradle position (Figure 15.4), lift the arm to throw-off at shoulder level and catch the club in the start position for the outward shoulder snake. Figure 14.1 (Lesson 14).

Downward - Begin a regular outward snake and travel down the body, again using the cradle position as the crucial transition point into an outward hip snake throw-off.

In order to master this trick, the two parts must be joined into one flowing movement. Now with two clubs try outward travelling body snakes in synchronous and then alternating time. Rest between attempts at gaining the smoothness that makes these involved movements so fascinating to watch. **Well done!**

Lesson 16
Inward Snakes

The last two lessons have described snakes in only the outward direction. It's time to learn shoulder and hip snakes the opposite way - inward. Inward snakes are more challenging, but with perseverance, you will accomplish these patterns. Learning snakes in both directions opens up a wide range of combinations including parallel snakes and will make it possible for you to adapt many classic wide swinging patterns with snake variations.

Inward Shoulder Snakes

This move is the twin of the regular outward snake as described in Lesson 14 (page 52). Refresh your memory of the outward full snake at shoulder level by performing it with both hands in synchronous time. The inward direction is the same trick in reverse order and the pattern again consists of two full circles followed by a throw-off.

Figure 16.1 Starting Position, Inward Snake

Hold a club in the snake grip, with your forefinger over the end of the knob (Figure 13.1, page 49). Figure 16.1 shows the starting position for the inward shoulder snake.

Check in a mirror that your elbow is in line with your shoulder and that the body of the club rests behind your upper arm. Your palm must be oriented inward, (toward your face) to begin the inward snake.

First Circle - Start the club in an arc inward, toward your head. The base of the club is brought up as the wrist turns down in front of your body and towards your chest. Figure 16.2.

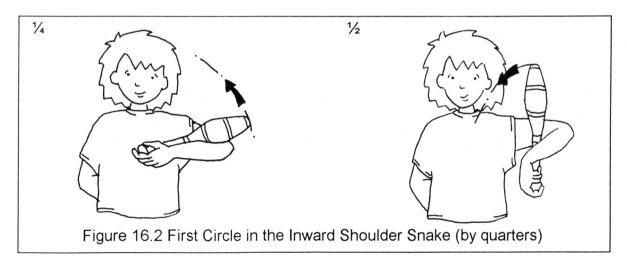

Figure 16.2 First Circle in the Inward Shoulder Snake (by quarters)

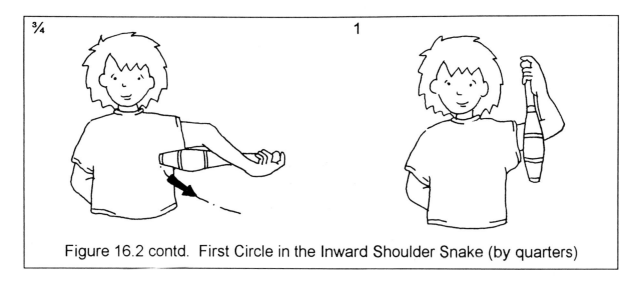

Figure 16.2 contd. First Circle in the Inward Shoulder Snake (by quarters)

It is very important to twist your palm toward your head before beginning the second circle.

Second Circle - Start position shown in the last picture of Figure 16.2 (1). Push the club inward and downward so that the club is forced under your elbow and behind your body. At the end of the second circle you are in the same position as for the start of an outward snake.

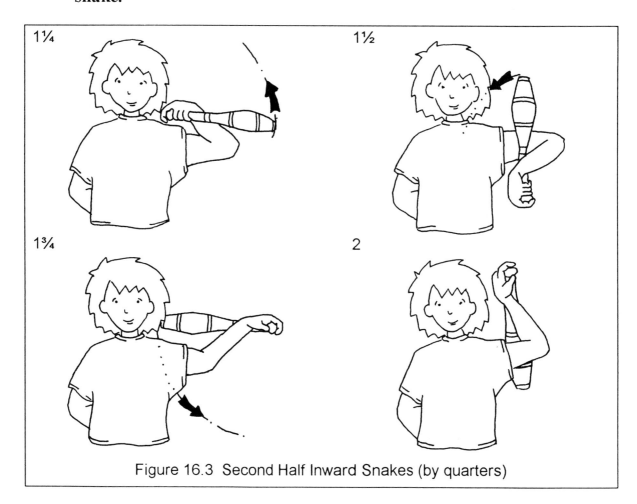

Figure 16.3 Second Half Inward Snakes (by quarters)

The second circle of the inward snake feels slightly peculiar because you seem to be "faking" (i.e., doing very little) while pushing the club behind the arm. A throw-off towards the head completes the inward shoulder snake and this is simply the reverse order of the throw-off shown in Figure 14.4, page 53.

Aim to keep your elbows high and in line with your shoulders when trying the following timings.

Synchronous time inward shoulder snakes.
Alternating time inward shoulder snakes.
Parallel snakes first to the left and then right.

Attempt to work both hands equally and gain a true balance of strength in your arm muscles. Movements involving continuous snakes may take quite a long time before they begin to feel smooth and comfortable. You should also recognise that alternating and parallel snakes are difficult patterns and expect them to take many hours to perfect.

Inward Hip Snakes

This is the twin move to the outward hip snake of Lesson 15 (page 56). Readers who have reached this far in the book will be experienced at reversing the direction of their club swinging patterns. Refresh your memory by performing synchronised outward hip snakes. Begin from a low cradle position (Figure 15.4, page 57), attempt the hip snake in the opposite direction by looking at the diagrams in Lesson 15 in backwards order. For inward hip snakes look at Figure 15.4, then 15.3, 15.2 and 15.1.

First Circle - The club head lowers inward and as you push your hand down and toward the outside of your body. Pull your hand up and the club will be held just underneath your forearm at the end of a small front circle. Figure 15.3, (1) on page 57.

The next part of the move will feel peculiarly like "cheating" as you push the club.

The forearm pushes down on the club to move it behind the body and ready for the throw-off at lower-back position. Figure 15.1, page 56.

A throw-off completes the inward hip snake and this is the reverse order of the diagrams in Figure 15.5 on page 58. Synchronous, alternating and parallel hip snakes are all possible. **Have fun experimenting!**

Lesson 17
Waist Circles and Waist Wraps

Intricate follow time patterns can be made around the waist. These tricks are difficult to explain and will take much practice to master. As well as reading this book, try to learn complicated movements from someone who can already smoothly perform them.

First warm up without the clubs. Include a special stretch with one arm behind your back and around your waist. Interlock this hand with the fingers of the other hand to gently pull the wrist forwards. Swap hands and repeat.

Waist Circles

There are a total of four different waist circles as they can be made in two directions, by each hand. These circles are formed at the waist and require the arms to stretch around the middle of your body.

Two Arm-Over-Back Waist Circles

Arm-over-back circles use the ring grip (Figure 3.2, page 15) with one hand stretched around the back of the waist.

With the right hand, place the arm behind your back, flat at waist level. Stretch to make outward circles at the front of the body on the front vertical plane - Figure 17.1. Keep the other hand out of the way by raising it.

This is an arm-over-back, outward front-waist circle. It is called a front-waist circle because the club is circling in front at waist level. Try this swing in the inward direction and with the left hand.

Figure 17.1 Arm-Over-Back, Outward Front-Waist Circle (right hand)

Still with just one hand, but now using the ball-and-socket grip (Figure 7.1, page 28) make circles behind the back. The club rotates close behind the arm at the back of the body and this pattern is called an arm-over-back, back-waist circle.

Keeping the arm behind the back, perform back-waist circles outward, then inward. These are circles behind the body with the arm stretched behind the waist. Swap hands.

Continuous waist circles will feel awkward at first. Move on to trying figure 8 patterns under-arm which swap between front and back-waist circles. These resemble the lower-front and back hand circles of Lesson 7 (page 31), except that now the arm is kept stretched behind the body along the waist line. Still with one hand alone swing:

Arm-over-back, outward, front and back-waist circles.
Arm-over-back, inward, front and back-waist circles.

Two Arm-Over-Front Waist Circles

Start with a single arm stretched across the front of your body (arm-over-front). Hold the club in a ring grip.

Individually rotate each club under the opposite arm and behind the body in the outward and then inward directions. Figure 17.2 shows an arm-over-front, inward back-waist circle.

Keep the other hand out of the way by raising it.

Practise the twin circle performed at the front of the body, the arm-over-front, front-waist circle. Link front and back moves to swing arm-over-front, front and back-waist figure 8 patterns.

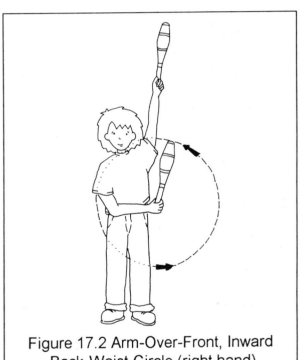

Figure 17.2 Arm-Over-Front, Inward Back-Waist Circle (right hand)

Still with the arm stretched along the front of the waist, swing circles at the front of the body, first in the outward and then the inward direction. Begin to change from the front to the back of your body, swinging front and back-waist figure 8 sweeps under the opposite arm.

Well done. Your wrists will be loosening up and becoming more flexible at performing circles close in around the waist.

Waist Figure 8's

Waist circles are linked with lower-front and back circles to form waist wraps. This first waist wrap pattern stays under one arm. It is most easily learnt in parallel time and then translated into the more lovely follow time pattern.

Stretch your left hand along your waist behind your back. With both hands, begin swinging outward, parallel circles under the right arm in figure 8's both in front and behind the back - Figure 17.3.

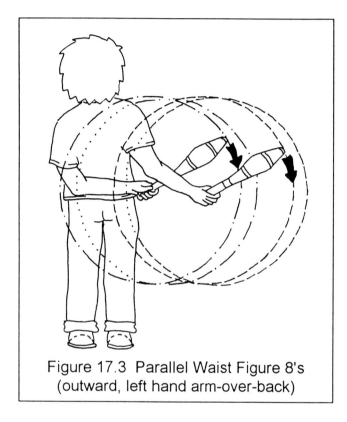

Figure 17.3 Parallel Waist Figure 8's
(outward, left hand arm-over-back)

Turn the clubs and wrists in and keep the back of the hand against your hip. (Figure 7.6, page 31.) Speed up the right hand to lead by half a circle in front of the left hand. This will bring the pattern into follow time.

Swing first the parallel and then follow time waist patterns inwards and with the right hand stretched behind the back. Learn them also with each arm-over-front in both the inward and outward directions. Be careful, but don't be surprised if you hit your elbows! I would suggest that you take a rest before learning the next pattern.

Back-Waist Wrap

The back-waist wrap is an impressive follow time pattern which moves across the back of the waist. It will feel strange to perform as it is asymmetrical. On the way across the back of the body there are a total of three circles as compared to just a single swing straight back to restart the motion, see Figure 17.4 opposite. It is best to learn this trick in parallel before performing the classic follow time movement. Use the ring grip.

With your left hand behind your back (Figure 17.3) begin a parallel, outward front-waist circle, moving into a circle directly behind the midline of the body and then an inward circle in front of the left side of your waist. Finally, you must swing straight across to begin an outward front-waist circle at front right position with the left hand behind the back.

Once you have the movement of three circles in parallel, change into follow time by speeding up the leading right hand, Figure 17.4. As a simplification only one trail is shown in the picture as the paths should more or less overlap. Try the trick in the opposite direction, i.e., beginning outward parallel circles on the left side of the body and also with the follow time wrap moving across the front of the body - a front-waist wrap.

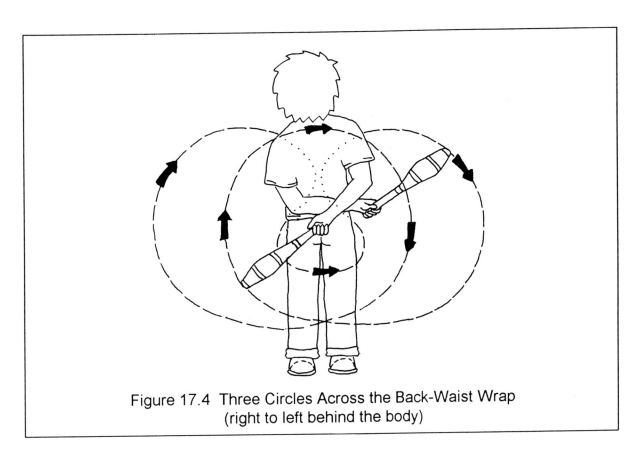

Figure 17.4 Three Circles Across the Back-Waist Wrap
(right to left behind the body)

Front-Waist Wrap

Front-waist wraps are made in exactly the same way as back-waist wraps, but with the three circles moving across the front of the body. Begin from swinging waist figure 8's with one arm stretched along the front of the waist. Introduce a circle in front of your navel and then an inward circle going behind the back before swinging across to restart the motion. As before, try the pattern in parallel before transferring into follow time.

Full-Waist Wrap

By linking together cycles of front and back-waist wraps it is possible to create a very beautiful club swinging movement that travels all the way around the waist. The full-waist wrap has a total of six circles, three in front and three behind the body, with each hand.

Directions are given for waist wraps moving from right to left. Use your right hand to lead this waist wrap while the left follows. Your right hand will always swing in the outward direction and the left in the inward direction.

The first step is to practise all six circles with each hand individually. Begin with your right hand on your right side and swing three outward lower-back circles - Figure 17.4. After completing three back circles travelling right to left, swing to return to the right side of the body and begin the three circles in a front-waist wrap (again moving right to left across). Learn to swing all six complementary inward circles around the waist with your left hand.

The adjustment from performing continuous back-waist wraps into swinging a full-waist wrap is made primarily by the follow hand, in this case the left. Your left hand leaves the normal back-waist wrap at the end of the third swing at the back left side of the body. This is the crucial position when the left hand must part from the other hand in order to move to the front right position. The left moves into an arm over-front, back-waist circle and is then rejoined with the right wrist.

Learn the full-waist wrap pattern in parallel time initially before speeding up the lead hand into the more lovely follow time movement.

Begin an outward, back-waist wrap from the right, as shown before in Figure 17.4. Link a front-waist wrap by using the left hand to move into an arm-over-front, back-waist circle, Figure 17.5.

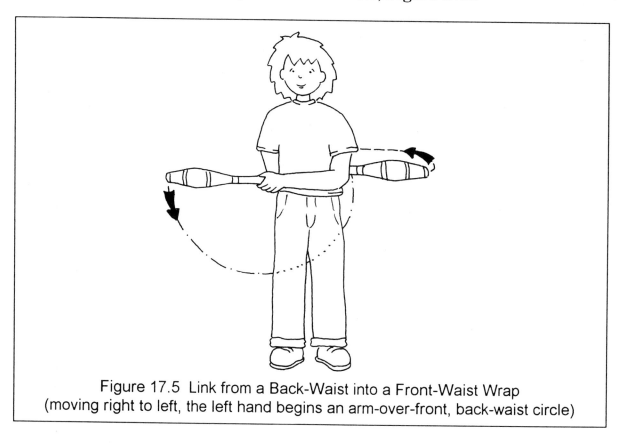

Figure 17.5 Link from a Back-Waist into a Front-Waist Wrap
(moving right to left, the left hand begins an arm-over-front, back-waist circle)

Now for the link from the front-waist wrap to return to swinging a back-waist wrap.

The right hand leads the pattern behind to restart the back-waist wrap. The left hand follows from the front of the body to the back around the waist and starts an arm-over-back, front-waist circle.

The full-waist wrap is not an intuitively easy pattern to grasp as there are so many layers of circles. Give it a few practice sessions and note that strong half-waist wraps are essential building blocks. But, once you have these elements, linking front and back-waist wraps in parallel and then follow time will lead to success. An advantage of the full-waist wrap over either front or back waist wraps is that the more complex pattern consisting of six follow time circles is symmetrical and therefore more flowing.

All waist wraps will look best if you keep your wrists closely together for the majority of the circles. Remember to try the pattern in both directions. **Good work.**

Lesson 18
Half and Full Fountains

Fountains incorporate both forward and backward cross-follow movements into dynamic patterns in follow time. These tricks are technically demanding, and yet, if you have read this far into the book you will have developed very supple wrists and these tricks are within your reach if you have a little determination.

Lower-Fountain

Low half fountains are a combination of forward and backward cross-follows performed just below the waist and flat to the front vertical plane. The pattern incorporates three positions for circles moving across the body. Look back at Lesson 11 (page 42) and retry the cross-follow movement in both the forward and backward directions.

With your feet always to the front, twist your body slightly to perform a forward cross-follow on the left side of the body. After the left hand has swung over the right, arc the right hand to the front so that the clubs are straight and horizontal as shown in Figure 18.1.

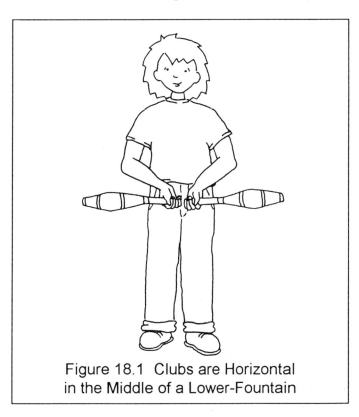

The figure shows the crucial change position between forward and backward cross-follows during a lower-fountain. At all times in the movement the clubs are in line as though they were one straight stick and the wrists stay glued close together.

Figure 18.1 Clubs are Horizontal in the Middle of a Lower-Fountain

From the position shown in Figure 18.1 move across to the right side of the body into a backward cross-follow by swinging the left hand under the right, now in the backward direction.

The change from a forward into a backward cross-follow is accomplished by each hand making a circle directly in front of the body. Figure 18.2 (over the page) shows the three positions for circles in the lower-fountain. The diagram is simplified to show the trail of only one club, as the paths will almost overlap.

Figure 18.2 Three Circles in the Lower-Fountain

Practise moving from backward into low forward cross-follows across the body, both with the right leading and then with the left hand leading (reverse the directions). Make sure that you can smoothly change directions. Try turning in a pirouette on the spot while swinging lower-fountains.

Prepare to add the upper fountain by opening the arms out into backward, alternating time full-arm circles. This pattern should flow out of the backward cross-follow, with a backward motion naturally travelling upwards. Move across the top of the body with a 180 degree turn overhead by following the high club down and into the forward direction (as for a full-arm pirouette, page 14.)

Upper-Fountain

This is a similar trick to the lower-fountain except that it is performed around the head and shoulders. Upper-fountains are slightly more difficult as high position changes of direction are tiring. First look back at the windmill as described in Lesson 12 (page 46) and swing the movement at least four times. The upper-fountain requires two further circles and these are made above each shoulder. I recommend trying opposite shoulder swings as a warm up.

Just with a single club in the right hand, swing upper-back circles over the opposite shoulder with your arm across the front of your body. Swing circles in both directions with each hand.

Next swing a series of 3 high circles across the body. It feels most natural to move up and across from a backward into a forward pattern. Start with an inward shoulder circle, then a mid-front circle directly over the head and finally an opposite shoulder swing down with a full-arm circle to start again. Try the 3 high circles with each hand and then with both in parallel time. The lead hand (inward) can then speed up slightly into follow time.

Figure 18.3 Opposite Shoulder Swing (right hand)

Swing a high backward, cross-follow on the right side of the body around your right shoulder. When the right hand swings over the left begin to move across the body in to the change position with both clubs horizontal, now in front of your face. This is a windmill in front of the head. Keep moving left to begin forward direction high cross-follows over the left shoulder.

Swing half full-arm circles down to restart the upper fountain again on the right side of the body. Repeat several times and then change direction so that the left hand leads the pattern across from left to right.

Full Fountain

Lower and upper fountains can be linked to form the classic full fountain. Figure 18.4 gives a simplified view of the full fountain which consists of six cross-follow patterns in a full circle around the body. There are twelve linked circular trails in the actual pattern.

It is easiest to swing backwards up and into an upper-fountain and forwards downward into a lower-fountain. The full fountain is stunning, but will take a great deal of practice until it is smooth, round and exactly flat to the front vertical plane.

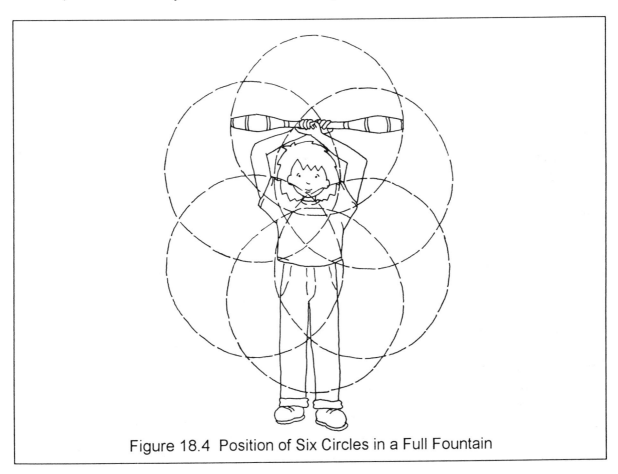

Figure 18.4 Position of Six Circles in a Full Fountain

I recommend that you work on the lower-fountain and once flowing, move the backward direction cross-follow up to shoulder level to begin an upper-fountain. Once you are able to move directly between upper and lower-fountains, you will have accomplished a full fountain. **Well done - you should feel very proud of yourself!**

Lesson 19
Essential Pole Moves

Club swinging and pole spinning are two closely related manipulation skills since they are both founded upon the development of strong, supple wrist motions. Three very useful pole spinning moves are described in this lesson. These central hold tricks will help you to put together a pole routine once linked with pole spinning adaptations of the club swinging movements you have already learnt.

I originally planned to write about the relationships between club swinging and pole spinning. But, since club swinging is a long subject in itself, a more comprehensive coverage of pole tricks will have to be published separately. My next book will include circular pole moves, off centre moves, twirling and placements, plus work with two poles. But, for now, this lesson's pole spinning relies on always holding the stick inside the hand - there is no twirling through the fingers.

Use a wooden broomstick, as these are cheap, strong and available from any DIY shop. A spearhead has been drawn to distinguish between the pole's two ends and is not compulsory. Wrap a coloured strip of tape around one end of your pole to help tell the ends apart.

A spinning pole can be thrown in many different ways. One of the most controlled methods is characterised as building speed and lift from a smooth one-handed rotation of the pole - the cradle rotation. First warm up and shake out your arms and wrists well.

Cradle Rotation
Hold the centre of the pole with your right hand so that it is horizontal in front of you with the knuckles on top. Loosen your grip slightly.

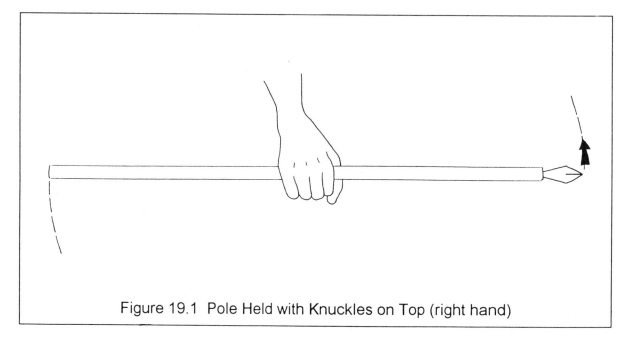

Figure 19.1 Pole Held with Knuckles on Top (right hand)

Turn your hand over 180° outwards - (i.e., right hand turn clockwise and left hand anticlockwise). The pole is now visible in the palm. Twist another 180° so that the pole has one end over the wrist as though you were cradling it - Figure 19.2 opposite.

70

After one complete circular spin, only the thumb is keeping the pole in place over the wrist in a cradle and this may feel uncomfortable at first. This pole cradle is directly analogous to the cradle position used when performing club swinging snake patterns see Figure 13.2 on page 49.

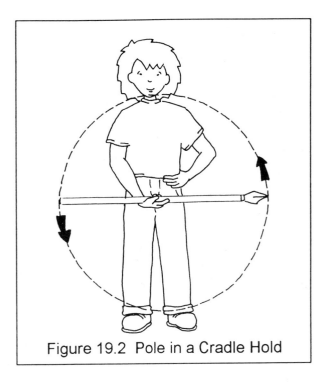

Figure 19.2 Pole in a Cradle Hold

Next, give a small lift while releasing the grip so that the pole leaves the hand and undergoes a 180° turn over the back of the wrist. Twist your hand inward to catch the middle of the pole again with a gentle snatch down as the pole completes a half circle.

You end the trick with a "knuckles on top" hold, as in Figure 19.1 but with the ends changed as the pole has undergone a rotation of 1½ spins. The crucial half spin is over the back of the wrist in the outward direction (thumb to little finger). Because the pole is always in contact with your hand, with practice, this method leads to a very reliable one handed spin. Try the cradle rotation with each hand turning outwards at the front, in the backwards direction and without looking at the pole.

The cradle rotation can be performed with two sticks in synchronous or alternating time, either outwards at the front (as described) or with a spin backward at the side of the body.

Throwing and Catching a Spinning Pole

From cradle position - Figure 19.2, increase the amount of lift when you let go so that the pole completes a half rotation in the air. Watch the spin and catch the pole when it is horizontal (knuckles on top - Figure 19.1) from above, if catching with the same hand, or else from below with the other hand.

Notice that if you catch with the other hand, you cannot immediately continue this outward spinning move. This is because the pole will be rotating the wrong way (i.e., inward instead of outward) to enter the cradle in that hand. Some intermediate move will be needed, such as the front propeller (page 72), to change hands or the direction of spin before starting another cradle. You could throw higher to make a full spin in the air, but mind your light bulbs if you try this trick inside! Extra speed and height can be gained by throwing just **before** the stick wraps around the wrist in a cradle. However, more control is then needed to make the flight take the desired path.

Front Propeller

To spin anticlockwise (from the audience viewpoint) first hold the centre of the pole in the left hand, upright, parallel to your legs (spear upright).

Turn the pole clockwise (inward) until it must almost travel over the back of the hand. At this point, the right hand reaches over the left hand and takes the pole just above the left hand in a "thumbs down", palm down grip - Figure 19.3.

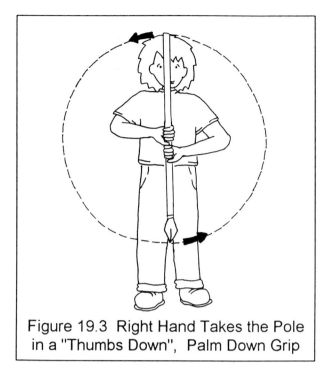

Figure 19.3 Right Hand Takes the Pole in a "Thumbs Down", Palm Down Grip

Introducing the right hand will make the spin steady. Try to continue using the momentum of the circle that has been started as the right hand spins the stick around for a full outward turn.

Release the left hand. The pole will then be twisted round by the right hand which will turn until the palm faces upwards. At this point, the left hand should reach under the right hand, palm up and take the pole Figure 19.4.

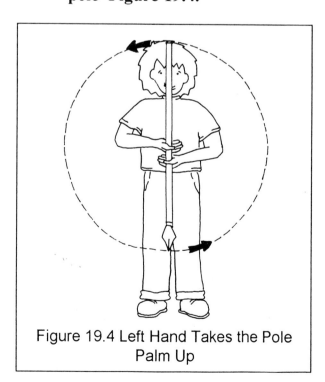

Figure 19.4 Left Hand Takes the Pole Palm Up

Each hand takes the pole in a grip that allows it to spin the pole around by **one full turn**. When one hand is released you must turn it around during the gap to allow maximum twist when that hand regains the pole.

Try also spinning the front propeller in the opposite direction (for a clockwise spin seen from the front swap hands and follow the instructions replacing right hand for left hand and vice versa). Change neatly between the two directions with a sharp stop when the pole is horizontal.

Lesson 20
Fancy Moves

High Throws

High throws are always spectacular. Use lightweight equipment and either throw just a single club or both. The number of spins made by the club in the air is determined by the amount of flick in your wrist as you throw.

First try throwing just one club with a single spin. You will have to watch the spin carefully to catch the handle rather than the head of the club and then allow your grip to slide down to the knob. Increase the height of the throw and the number of spins up to 4 or 5 spins. Swap hands and then try to throw two clubs at once.

When two clubs are collected and stacked in one hand before being launched together, this double throw is known as a 'multiplex'.

Body Throws

There are a range of trick throws around the body that can be integrated with club swinging. These include throwing a club under the leg, behind the back, over the top, with any number of spins and even side or reverse spin.

Juggling Three Clubs While Also Club Swinging

Club juggling usually involves the manipulation of three clubs and you will be able to find a juggling text book or someone to explain the basic cascade pattern. Many jugglers find that club swinging is a perfect warm up to juggling. There is also the advantage that swinging can be a very useful method of keeping a performance going if one of the clubs is dropped.

The easiest way of bringing in club swinging into a juggling routine is to catch two clubs in one hand and then swing both clubs as if they were a single club. However, the most common method of mixing swinging with juggling is to juggle two clubs in one hand while club swinging independently with the other hand e.g. two in the left hand while swinging lower-front and back circles with the right hand.

The forward cross-follow (page 42) is one pattern where three clubs can be juggled and swung together. I understand that the 'spare' club must be thrown from the hand that is underneath. It should travel straight up with a slow double spin. The clubs change around with one club always in the air on the outside of the pattern. I am still working on this!

Swinging With 4 Or 6 Clubs

Although much more tiring, it is possible to club swing with more than just a single club in each hand. The grips alter as you will need to stack the clubs. This restricts freedom over the range of tricks as you cannot change grip. However, alternating patterns usually work well.

For two clubs in each hand, one fits in the normal place between finger and thumb Figure 1.3, (page 8). The other knob rests in the palm and is held by the last two fingers so that it points in the opposite direction to the first. A second club should not go between any of the other fingers. To add a third club, place it in the gap between your middle and ring fingers.

Beating - Hitting Equipment Together

Deliberately knocking either clubs or poles together is called beating. By introducing an audible sound from your equipment you can bring life and surprise into a performance. It is very useful when choreographing a routine, since beating is an effective method of tightly, and noticeably, fitting movements to the music. Beating adds interest as it is largely unexpected. Variations include beating the clubs of a partner, domino effects, knocking two clubs together in the same hand and group beats set by clubs drummed against the floor. To succeed, the hitting must be very controlled and you must remember to keep a sense of symmetry throughout the whole of your body. Otherwise, it may seem as if the tapping were an unintended mistake!

Beating poles together will be louder than clubs. Different sounds will be heard depending upon the material - e.g. wood, metal or bamboo. A crashing sound may be frightening, which adds excitement to your show. Alternatively, you could aim for creating a pattern with an interesting rhythm, for instance, tap dancing with a walking stick.

In some Peking Opera scenes the warriors slap the ends of their spear against their own upturned feet and use various parts of their body to deflect or kick the spears thrown by opponents. I would not recommend that you try these moves with an ordinary broomstick. They are possible without injury mainly because of the flexible nature of the ratan sticks preferred by traditional Chinese pole spinners.

Balancing Equipment

Add further dimensions to your swinging performance by integrating balancing movements. It is possible to place the base of the club on the floor and lean weight upon it in order to, for instance, lift one leg high and swing a pattern underneath with the free club.

Alternatively, a club could be balanced with the knob placed on your chin or forehead. This will take some practice and the skill relies on watching the top of the club and making many small movements with your neck to compensate for any tilting of the club. Balancing is easier with long objects and with objects that are top heavy.

Rolling

Your clubs or other equipment could be made to roll along the ground, adding a slow aspect to your routine. Rolled clubs will form an arc on the floor and the push-off into the roll must be very controlled for the movement to work.

Placements and Carries

Some advanced swinging movements rely on placing the clubs on parts of the body and then letting go while the clubs rest or are carried for a short while. Examples are where forward swings are used to place clubs on the back of the shoulders which are dipped down to the horizontal plane. Release your grip just before lifting your shoulders to make the clubs bounce up and the clubs are then caught in front of the body.

The neck, elbows, hips and knees are other possible positions for placements where the club is temporarily released from the hand. Placements include movements where clubs are carried from the back to the front of the body whilst held only by the elbow. These very individual movements are best learnt through experimentation - have fun!

Club Swinging Problems and Solutions

Finding something tough? Use this chapter as a reference guide when you are experiencing any difficulty. Look down the following list for the problem and consider if the suggested solution is appropriate. The answers are mostly common sense. Make use of these tips to achieve greater progress with your club swinging.

Strains

Painful, but not uncommon for those who throw themselves straight into a hard practice session without any preparation. Identify the strained muscle or sprained joint. You will probably need to rest it for a few hours if not days. Gentle massage may aid the healing.

In future, do not be so impatient to practise. Always warm up the weak area with special care and go easy on it until the strength is fully regained. Another tip is to specifically tailor your warm up to flex those areas with stiffness or where you have had difficulty in the past.

Club swinging has been used as a physiotherapy exercise to strengthen and cure joints with injuries. Perhaps the strain was caused by mishandling heavy loads or by some other activity, in which case, gentle swinging will heal and firm up the muscles.

Hitting Yourself

Learning a new move will often involve dealing with a few knocks to your body. Do not be put off by the first badly placed swing. **Slow down and learn from it.** Where did it hit and why?

Q) Were you going too quickly to keep control?
A) Slow right down before building up speed, now with improved control.

Q) Did you lose concentration?
A) Regain your focus by looking straight ahead at a distant spot. If this does not work, then take a short break.

Q) Was it due to inflexibility in any particular joint?
A) Work on this joint with warm up exercises before attempting the move again, with improved suppleness and reach.

Q) Were you transferring unsuccessfully from one move to another?
A) Plan the transition so that it flows. The change you are attempting may not be working because your timing needs adjustment.

Q) Was it because you were stepping in an incompatible direction?
A) If so, then rethink the twist or steps and try the move again.

Bruising

If knocks are hard, or repeated, then bruising may result. Analyse which particular trick is causing painful hits. Accept the warning signal from your body's defences and take a rest from the move that is damaging.

If the bruising warrants it, take some ice or frozen vegetables from the freezer and make an ice pack to numb the tender area. Arnica ointment may also help.

Accidentally Hitting Others

Very embarrassing and to be avoided at all times or else you will lose friends. Always apologize before considering if it was your fault.

Q) Were you standing too close to them, i.e. less than an arm's length away?
A) **Always check that you have enough room** in all directions before beginning to club swing. Warn those people that you commonly practise around of the dangers of getting in the way. Children, in particular, often come too close for comfort.

Q) Did a club inadvertently fly off at speed?
A) This loss of grip is a symptom of loss of concentration. Collect the errant club. Have a rest and then go slowly, taking care not to be over-confident when there are others around who could get hurt.

Q) Did the clubs knock together before flying off?
A) Probably a good thing in terms of slowing down the impact. But, where and why did they collide? See the following section on clubs colliding.

Clubs Colliding

Take a moment to consider at what point, and why, did the clubs collide?

Make sure that you allow the clubs to pass one another by:

- swinging one hand in front of the other, or
- widening the distance between the clubs, or
- trying the pattern in a different timing before returning to the move that caused a collision.

Q) Did you lose concentration?
A) Regain your focus before continuing.

Q) Is it really feasible to perform this move without a collision?
A) If not, then perhaps it is possible to turn a gentle beating of the clubs to your advantage - for instance a domino effect or an opportunity for comedy. Look at the sections on beating in Lesson 20, page 74.

Sore Hands

A committed club swinger may suffer from sore hands following heavy practice over successive days. This is a natural consequence if you are aiming at rapid progress. The sore points can be eased by the use of a moisturising cream. Eventually your skin will toughen up.

If you are using a fuel (paraffin is recommended), for fire club swinging, it is worth cleaning your hands carefully after packing away. This helps prevent the fuel from causing a rash to develop on already sore areas.

Blistering

Blistering is most often a sign of poor grip. Make sure that the knob of the club is not in between the fingers. It should be held in the notch between thumb and first finger.

Preferably, the knobs on your clubs should be both rounded and smooth. They must be firmly attached to the clubs, so tighten the screws if they are loose. Protect the blistered area from further rubbing with a plaster and take a rest.

Uneven Circles

If your patterns are producing ovals or ellipses rather than circles, you have poor swinging planes. Watching yourself practise in a mirror and making adjustments is the best cure.

Q) Is one hand worse than the other?
A) Work hardest with the weaker hand, practising with it alone until planes are flat to the front.

Problems with Alternating Timing

This is a difficult timing and so practise the move with your weak hand alone until it is smooth. Bring in the stronger side whenever it feels right to do so. Continue the move with the subdominant side and let strongest hand find the rhythm. With practice your coordination will improve until both sides are equally strong.

Problems with Parallel Movements

Parallel movements require both arms and hands to be equally flexible. Keep the movement flat to the correct swinging plane.

Q) Are you going faster with one hand?
A) Slow right down so that you can control the dominant hand.

Q) Is one hand much weaker?
A) Practise with the weak hand alone for 8 counts slowly and 8 counts at faster speed.

Problems with Patterns in Follow Time

Follow time patterns are demanding and so require much practice to master. Begin in parallel then slightly speed up the lead hand until it is a half a circle in front of the other hand. Note that strong parallels are a prerequisite to learning good follow time patterns.

Sometimes you may not believe that you can do a trick correctly when, in reality, you have accomplished the move, although still only in a rough form. Ask someone who is able to do the pattern to look at your follow time swinging moves.

Problems with Snakes

Snakes are tricks that take a fair amount of work to perform with any fluidity. This is because the club does not swing with gravity, but must be directed around the arm using a limber wrist. Watch the movement of the snake in a mirror and keep the pattern high and flat to the plane. It may be that you are performing snakes but that you do not realise it! This is because snakes feel very awkward until you have practised them for some time.

Putting Together A Routine

Placing moves in an ordered sequence will greatly improve your presentation skills. Spend time on a short routine because you will learn that smooth transitions between your patterns are **as important** as the individual tricks themselves. The instructions are mostly common sense and are widely applicable to club swinging, pole spinning, juggling and many other performance arts.

Motivation
Set a **goal date**, e.g., a friend's birthday party, for which you want to have a completed routine. Fixing a deadline and reason for the routine is a fantastic aid to motivation, but be realistic and start planning between a month and a week before the event.

Consider the Audience
The intended audience will enjoy your performance all the more if it is tailored to them. Are they children/adults, sitting/standing? Is the routine in the context of a show, or perhaps busking outside? Are you working alone or in a group, with music or words and with what kind of lighting? You may not know all the answers to these questions, but use your best guess and common sense. You will often be able to choose many of these variables.

Listing Your Repertoire of Tricks
- First write down a list of all the different props you could use in a show, including clubs, a pole, juggling props, musical instruments and comedy items.
- Next write down a full list of all the tricks that you can reliably do in no particular order. Make up titles for any that are not yet named.
- Then, asterisk all those tricks that will impress the intended watchers. "Funny" or "unusual/surprising" moves generally fall into this category. Technical tricks may not appeal to the general public as much as fast moves or body tricks like under the leg.
- Next, highlight those moves that you enjoy or find rewarding.
- Cross off any tricks that would be ineffective under the conditions that you have chosen (e.g., club swinging snakes can be dangerous with fire).
- **Warm up**. Check that you really can do all the listed tricks reliably by rehearsing each at least 10 times in succession. Strike out those patterns that do not pass the test. This process will yield a repertoire of your own performable standard tricks.

Music
Working a routine to music is generally a good idea (excepting slapstick comedy) as music will aid rhythm, set a pace and bring depth to your show. **Choose your music with care.**

I advise a piece without many words as these will detract from your skill. It is very important to pick music that you enjoy. You will need to listen to the tune many, many times if you are to choreograph your routine at all closely! The music should also be accessible to the listeners and appropriate for the mood of your routine. For instance, oriental pieces will give a mystic feel, dramatic music is best if you decide to act out a fight and comedy routines are enhanced by the use of music that has a surprising or amusing content.

If you are not knowledgeable about music, persuade a friend who is to offer suggestions. Asking an expert can save a lot of time and searching. Be sure to record your cassette to a high quality.

The Start and Finish Tricks

Knock them dead with an attention-grabbing first trick that absolutely must be one that you can land successfully **every time**. After this confident start, your show should build to a finale, which again, is spectacular and yet **completely reliable**. Write down the first and last moves now as chosen from the asterisked tricks.

The Middle Tricks

From your repertoire list, provisionally order only three other tricks into a sequence that develops. Aspire to make the transitions among these three as good as they can be. Ball jugglers should avoid doing the simple cascade between tricks, and endeavor to coordinate moves with pleasing changes. A mirror will help a great deal. When repeating a trick, four times (or an even number) is advisable since music tends to have four beats per bar. Try the short sequence until you have rehearsed it **reliably** 10 times.

Do not be over-ambitious. If it is too difficult, cut the hardest move and replace it with something that is easily within your level of ability. Continue to add single tricks to either end of the existing three trick sequence, given that you have predefined the start and finish.

The Routine

When you have between 6-10 tricks listed in an order, with graceful transitional moves, start to rehearse with your music or comedy. Rearrange the sequence until the two parts (visual and audio) match well, e.g., on high notes give height and present 'funny' tricks with an amusing introduction. Include some surprises, delight in your own imagination and the unexpected!

Short routines are always better than too long, so do not be afraid to fade out the music, even down to as little as 1-2 minutes. Cut the least interesting parts and shuffle the rest again so that the routine peaks to a climax. Practise an entrance and a bow in order to round off your show professionally.

Finishing Touches

Your routine is nearly ready. Prepare early to allow enough time to rehearse it well.
- Consider ways of dealing with any mistakes (e.g., spare props/'floor' juggling and comedy 'drop lines').
- Think about costume and make-up to enhance your character.
- Show the routine to someone whose opinion you value for comments.
- Make any minor amendments to polish your show, then time the entire routine.
- Reward yourself somehow (e.g., with a trip to the fridge).
- Rewind the tape and get your equipment ready.
- To be at your best, warm up before **energetically** presenting the routine.

Routine Check List

Date .... Time ....
Place ....
Solo /Group routine .... for audience of Adults / Children / Mixed
Equipment / Props List ....
Costume .... Music by ....
Scripted YES / NO Title or theme ....
Total Length .... Special effects ....

Fire Performance and Safety

Displays of fire torch swinging look great! The flames leave dramatic patterns behind them against the darkness and it was the circular trails of torches that inspired me to learn club swinging. Fortunately, it is not that much more difficult to swing fire torches than ordinary clubs, except that **you must constantly bear safety in mind**.

Fire torches can be bought from juggling retailers - see the equipment chapter on pages 89-90 for details. Torches designed for fire juggling or fire swinging are both equally good provided that there is a knob firmly attached. Before trying your torches lit, get used to practising with them unlit in daylight. Next try swinging them lit in daylight. Particularly if you want to throw and catch the torches, when you first start to manipulate lit torches at night, make sure you are close to a source of light to see the handles of the clubs.

It is a good idea to wear a hat and tie long hair back. You should take off loose clothing, warm up and ensure that there is sufficient space around you before beginning your practice session. Always practise fire outside, in a clear area well away from buildings, vehicles, tents or other flammable objects.

Safe Fuels

Use paraffin (or kerosene). Paraffin can be bought from selected petrol filling stations and hardware stores. This fuel is coloured blue or pink, burns with a yellow flame and gives off quite a lot of smoke. Barbecue lighter fluid is an alternative. It is more expensive and burns hotter than paraffin but with less smoke. Coleman fuel (an American brand name) can also be used. This is a proprietary fuel made for the Coleman Company, an American camping equipment firm. It is basically naphtha, also called white gas (although it is **not** unleaded petrol). Its equivalent is available in the UK and Germany, for instance 'Shell' stations sell it as SBP4. These recommended fuels have cool flames. If you accidentally catch the torch at the lit end, or if you drop the club on yourself it will not immediately burn you.

Watch where you left the container of fuel - which should be a manufactured metal or plastic fuel container. Clearly mark the container with the words 'Highly Inflammable'. Never use a jam jar or drinks container to store or carry fuel. Keep your fuel away from where you will light, swing or juggle the fire torches.

Fuel containers should be kept closed at all times, unless actually being poured.

Never use petrol as a fuel, it burns much hotter than paraffin and its vapour is explosive!
Never use meths (methanol). Meths is methylated alcohol or methylated spirits. It is about 90% ethanol which is made poisonous by the deliberate addition of methanol. Do not use it as it can damage the optic nerve in the human eye!

Fuelling Up

Pour enough paraffin into an open-topped metal container (e.g., metal bucket or tin) to just cover the wick of the torch. Dip the torch and wait long enough to allow excess fuel from the torches to drain back into the container. Once you have dipped the torch wick, always vigorously **shake off excess fuel before you light up**. This should be away from where you are going to perform or practise. Remembering to shake off before lighting a fire torch is very important. If you leave an excess of fuel on the wicks it will fly off while you swing.

Lighting the Torches

Paraffin needs to be quite hot before it will ignite and you may have to hold a match to the wick for up to ten seconds. Once one torch is lit, others may be lit from it. A fire torch will burn for up to five minutes. Stand so that any wind will blow the flames away from you. While you are not actually moving lit torches, hold them upward, so that the flames do not burn the handles or your hands! Remember that heat always rises.

Fire Club Swinging

Fire swinging looks best against a dark background. Wide swinging patterns and those that are fast enough to produce fully circular trails are often the most successful moves. But, I would not recommend attempting snakes unless you can do them very fast and are wearing fire resistant clothing.

Putting the Torches Out

In order to keep your torches in prime condition, they should be blown out or smothered with a damp natural fibre cloth or fire blanket before going out of their own accord. The torches should then be re-dipped in fuel, drained, shaken off and left to cool in a safe place.

When clearing up, pour any unused fuel back into the storage container with a funnel. All equipment should be wiped clean of traces of paraffin with newspaper or a rag cloth which should immediately be put in a dustbin.

Care of Torches

Maintain your torch wicks, making sure that they are firmly attached to the torch body. The screws holding the wick should be tight, but take care not to over-tighten. Similarly, the screw holding the knob on to the other end of the torch should be regularly tested before use and tightened if necessary. If you repeatedly re-light your torches while they are still hot you will greatly shorten the life of the clubs because they suffer increased heat.

Safety Summary

Fire club swinging is not a dangerous activity if you use your common sense and follow the procedures. However, it is essential to seek expert advice if you are staging a large event as crowd control, fire prevention, first aid, and emergency procedures are all complex issues.

- Warm up thoroughly.
- Wear a hat or tie long hair back and remove any loose clothing.
- Fire swing outdoors, away from potentially flammable objects.
- Use paraffin (kerosene) and thoroughly shake off excess fuel before the torches are lit.
- Secure the lid of the marked fuel container before you begin the show.
- Watch the wind and stand so that the flames blow away from you.
- Warn an audience that it is real fire and therefore dangerous. Tell them that they are not to come closer than a specified safety distance (a minimum of three meters). If busking with fire, define a line which the public cannot cross by the use of a rope.

Never use petrol or meths.
Never use fire if you have drunk any alcohol as your reactions will be too slow for safety.

Simple First Aid

The following paragraph applies to small burns and unbroken skin. More complex injuries should always be referred to medical aid because of possible infection, loss of fluids, shock or other complications.

For minor skin burns, first remove any clothing covering the affected area. Place the bare skin under cold running tap water for **at least 10 minutes**. Wrap the tender area with the cleanest material available.

Mass Fire Swinging Routine

I was asked to write and teach a fire swinging routine for presentation at the 16th European Juggling Convention. The central idea was to involve many club swingers from different nations in a mass, synchronised fire show. After just a few rehearsals the following large-scale routine was performed by 29 fire swingers, all of whom I would like to thank for their skill and enthusiasm. Thanks also to the fantastic hand drummers who accompanied us. As the entire routine is quite short (4 minutes), we decided to perform it twice, at either end of the outdoor arena and just before and after the firework display.

The routine is pitched at an intermediate level. Where moves are especially difficult, you may want to substitute a similar pattern. Most music has 4 beats to the bar and you should **repeat each sequence in 4:4 time.** The count is given down the right side of the page. It represents the number of times to repeat full combinations and you should count just from the right hand (RH). Hints are given after the routine.

If you decide to learn and perform a mass show with other fire swingers, then be aware of each other to keep your patterns synchronised. This routine contains a repositioning of the people (the floor pattern) between sections. The idea is to walk confidently as you change places. The performers begin facing the audience in a wide line, then walk into two circles looking inward. Section C is then swung with people standing in deep lines behind each other. The finale, which consists mainly of parallel movements towards the middle of the performance space, is designed to focus the attention of the audience as the routine closes.

Equipment: 2 torches each, paraffin fuelled, shaken and lit backstage **just before** the show.
Entrance: Each person has two clubs held high and crossed above their head whilst beating the clubs together (see page 73). Form neat lines facing the audience and give everyone room. Wait with your arms in start position, clubs held straight up at chest level.

Beats/Revolutions

Start: Section A

Walking Intro: 20

1 RH (right hand) solo full-arm circles INWARDS. Stop high in start position.	4
2 OUTWARD full-arm circles together in synchronous time.	4
3 Synchronous upper-front & shoulder circles.	4
3a Transition: double up two outward upper-front hand circles.	
4 Alternating outwards, short reel done up high. Use a wide arm swing down to:	4
5 Popular outwards reel (combination full-arm and shoulder circles, alternating).	Fast 8
6 Short reel low (alternating lower-front & backs)	4
7 Short reel low with circles **doubled up** front and then back.	4
8 PARALLEL figure 8 hand circles inside & outside-the-arms forwards to the front.	

Floor Pattern

Walk into a CIRCLE floor pattern while swinging parallel figure 8 hand circles.　　16
Face inwards to the circle. "X" denotes a performer with 12 people shown in the example.

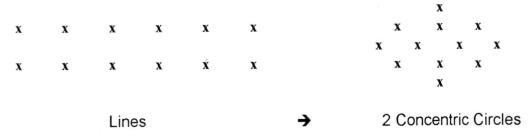

Lines　　　　　　　　　➜　　　2 Concentric Circles

We waited until people were evenly spaced in the circles before beginning the middle section. Check the distance between you by spreading your arms out into a star.

Middle: Section B

9	Synchronous time forward hand circles outside-the-arm to touch the ground.	8
10	Backward hand circles back up high.	8
	Repeat 9, 10 with cross-overs between synchronous hand circles outside-the-arms.	16
11	Begin with RH, alternating, backwards full-arm circles.	4
11a	Transition: slow half pirouette turning R, when R club is high.	
12	Facing outwards from the circle, alternating forwards full-arm circles.	4
13	Full pirouette to face outwards straight into:	
14	Cross-follow forwards FAST.	4
15	Circles split in half from the front. Walk with a cross-follow to new floor pattern four PARALLEL LINES DOWN (at least 6 feet apart, clubs in start position).	16

Floor Pattern

Walk from the circles into deep parallel lines facing the audience.

2 Circles	→	Parallel Lines Down

Finale: Section C

16	PARALLEL lower-front & full-arm circles towards middle of lines (i.e.R line left).	8
17	Two slow full-arm parallel turns.	4
18	Parallel swing of leading hand between legs (lower backs, full-arm circles). Finish in start position.	4
19	Synchronous time, outward full-arm and shoulder circles. Stop high.	8
20	**TOGETHER** Beat floor shouting "HUH", rise quickly up to finish with arms out in a star. **Statue for 4 counts.** Collect torches in RH. Walk to form two long LINES ACROSS facing audience.	

Bow twice, taking cue from mid person. Then slowly walk off from the end of the line.

Fortunately the routine is much easier to perform than it is to read. However, I recognise that there are some slightly tricky aspects which need some explanation.

Hints on Section A - Moves in Synchronous and Alternating Time

The first difficult change is from synchronous time upper-front and shoulder circles into the same high pattern but in alternating time (3a Transition). Practise the change by performing just upper-front hand circles with your right hand and then adding an occasional single upper-back circle. Lesson 8 presents other exercises that will help you to learn how to change between timings. In particular, you should try the move shown in Figure 8.1, page 33.

The next difficult change is to double up the timing on the lower-front and back hand circles, which is move number 7. Do the movement with just a single hand to get the wrist to swing two (rather than just one) circle both at lower-front and back positions.

Hints on Section B - Forward and Backward Directions

This section has two difficult aspects. The first is to rise up from the ground with backward cross-over circles. Expect the backward direction to feel awkward at first, but it becomes smoother after a little practice.

Perhaps the most flashy movement in this section is the full pirouette into the forward cross-follow. Practice full-arm pirouettes as explained on page 14 in order to learn a neat turn.

Hints on Section C - Parallel Movements

When performers are positioned behind each other and deep on to the audience, the effect of club swinging is greatly enhanced. The people directly in front appear to have many arms!

The most difficult transition in the final section is to swing between the legs and then change from parallel movements to an outward, synchronous time pattern. We stopped briefly at starting position to make the timing adjustment.

A loud "HUH" a the end is a signal to the audience that the routine is over and that they should start to cheer. This applause cue is reinforced by the stillness of performers as they statue in a star for 4 counts.

It is safer to alter a normal bow slightly so that the still lit torches are placed on the ground rather than in the air. Wait to blow out the torches at the side of the performance area.

Ultraviolet (uv) Performance

Performances using ultraviolet (uv) light are mesmerizing to watch. Under ultraviolet light (black light), a performer moving brightly coloured equipment can create optical traces in the paths of objects. The trails left by fluorescent props in motion are both stunning and fairly easy to produce. All that is really required to get an effect is that performers are close enough to the uv light source(s) for fluorescent objects to appear brighter than the background. If near, or ideally complete, darkness is available the effects are greatly enhanced. By blacking out all of yourself, the objects you are controlling can appear to move through the air of their own accord - creating the greatest potential for optical illusion.

Fluorescent Equipment

Juggling manufacturers are producing an ever expanding range of uv equipment. There are basically two sorts of professional props: those that are fluorescent, or 'day glow' and these will be brightly coloured, as compared to luminous or 'glow-in-the-dark' equipment which is always a pale shade of yellow or green.

Luminous juggling kit is manufactured so that it can be charged under a normal light, such as a desk lamp. When all the lights are switched off, the specialist material releases stored energy and the props will emit a green coloured 'glow'. Fully luminous balls and clubs can shine for some time once charged with a normal bulb but are brightest (and last longer) if charged under an ultraviolet light. The fact that they visibly glow from all directions is an advantage for routines involving toss juggling as no back lighting will be required (i.e., lights behind the performer).

There is more choice of colours in fluorescent as opposed to luminous props. Choose clubs in the 'day glow' range of colours (e.g., shocking pink or orange). Fluorescent pigments are usually very visible in sunlight and they will also be bright in uv. However, the coloured fluorescent clubs will not actually 'glow-in-the-dark' and so fluorescent props can only be seen well when lit from the front or above. Because fluorescent colours do not emit light, if you want to throw and catch these props then some back lighting is essential.

An alternative to using the standard manufactured fluorescent equipment is to design and make your own props to suit your show. Use fluorescent paints, paper, bright tapes and, perhaps even trains of ribbons to add a unique style to your equipment. I have found that clear sticky plastic is good at protecting home decorations.

Ultraviolet Light Fittings and a Protective Cage

Professional sound and lighting hire shops will be able to supply ultraviolet lights of the sort used in discotheques. These purple tinted bulbs are completely harmless to human eyes and will not tan the skin. UV performance is safer and much cleaner than fire. Ultraviolet lighting tubes are most commonly available in 4 foot lengths. The bulbs are usually 40 Watt and can be fitted into standard ceiling lighting fittings. You will probably need illumination from more than one side to fully bathe a stage and some back lighting is essential for performers themselves to see fluorescent props, although luminous or 'glow-in-the-dark' props are visible from all sides, once charged.

Black light tubes are much more expensive than normal white fluorescent tubes and are very easily broken. Both are good reasons to protect your lights from fallen equipment and during transportation. Cages are not usually available commercially, so you (or a friend who has tools and spare time) will need to construct one. An example is to individually house your lights in a guttering or plastic pipe sawn in half long ways. Attach a large piece of centimeter square wire mesh over the bulb by fixing it inside the cage with nuts and bolts. Standard lighting tube fittings are used and these often come supplied with a white bulb, which you could safely be rid of by giving it back to the shop. Ask someone who is good at wiring to help check the electrical safety of the fitting and plug.

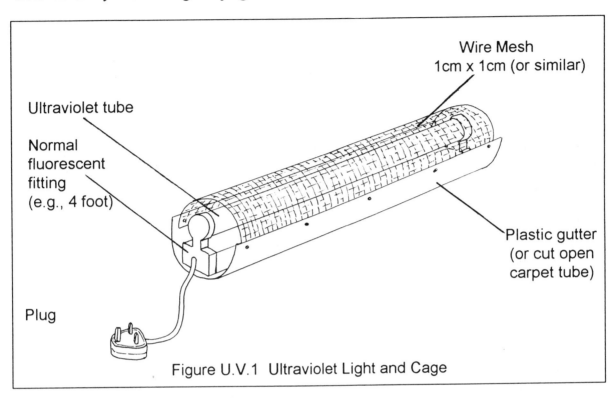

Figure U.V.1 Ultraviolet Light and Cage

Costumes

A dark backdrop is highly recommended for any show involving black light. If you want the audience to focus on the patterns of your uv props, then performers should wear all black clothing. If you aim to create optical illusions, such as puppetry effects or levitation, it is important that performers can not be seen at all. However, it is worth remembering that complete black out is difficult to achieve in non-theatre venues and this will restrict the number of performance occasions in which the people will be fully invisible.

If your show includes dance, pirouettes or 'body tricks' then a partly fluorescent costume will pick out the relevant features of your body. Washing clothes in a soap powder containing optical brighteners is one method of making light colours show up under uv. Spending time designing and making a proper uv costume is worthwhile if you have a particular style in mind. Many arts and crafts shops sell fluorescent fabric paints and combining with these with fluorescent materials sewn onto a basic dark costume can highlight your body's outline. The costume should not be more visible than your equipment or it may detract from your skills. Fluorescent face paints can be applied indicate your facial features such as eyes, mouth, nose and, even ears. Wearing a mask is also an option.

Music

Ultraviolet light tends to mask the performer while heightening the effects of moving equipment. These are some of the reasons why many uv shows are often choreographed to music rather than to spoken comedy. Music should be recorded to a high quality and be accessible to the intended audience - see the chapter on putting together a routine on page 78.

UV Routines

With fully luminous props (such as glowing clubs) it is possible to turn the lights off for parts of a show. This will only work if the equipment is previously well charged. Often more successful is to work in a dark room, with pure ultraviolet lighting through out. The uv will make 'day glow' colours brighter and will continuously charge luminous props whilst also keeping any performers wearing full black out hidden.

To make striking images, I believe that the motion of props under ultraviolet light needs to be both graceful and well defined. Stand side on to perform moves in the side vertical plane, so that the audience can see a fully circular pattern. If your equipment goes behind any part of your body (e.g., between the legs or behind the waist) then it may cause a brief silhouette. This will affect the visual flow of the movement because the prop will be momentarily hidden. I have seen this used for comic effect as though the clubs are 'hiding' from view.

Remember that when club swinging, the club retraces its path and often catches up with its own trail. To reinforce continuous patterns the clubs must exactly follow their previous path. If the props collide or there is a hesitant stop, the audience will certainly notice.

My personal approach is that ultraviolet routines are most entertaining when they are dynamic, fast moving and high energy. Just as with any show (be it with fire, normal clubs or whatever) it is the accelerating or unexpected tricks that will have most effect. Contrast these with some slower and more graceful movements, remembering that the visual appeal of the patterns is more important than the individual tricks. Gain speed towards the end of the routine to finish with your most astounding move and give your audience the colourful optical trails that they most want to see.

UV Performance Summary

- Low power ultraviolet light is safe and clean, when compared with fire.
- Use a uv light from a sound and lighting shop, never a sun bed light (which will tan).
- Cage your ultraviolet light to protect the tube.
- Luminous props always glow green whilst fluorescent equipment can be any colour.
- Remember to take a black backdrop and an extension cable to your bookings.
- If you decide to do a show outdoors, check that your electric cables are waterproof.
- Warn people that you are going to turn out the lights for your show so that they can find their belongings before the room goes dark.
- Just before the show, shut out or switch all normal light sources (except Exit signs).
- Apart from theatre venues, full black out is rarely available. Illusions will not work every time.
- Leave the ultraviolet light on throughout the uv routine.
- The performer will not be able to reliably throw and catch non-luminous equipment unless there is some back lighting.
- As always, warm up before performing.

Equipment

Clubs - Manufactured by Juggling Companies

Major juggling shops have a wide variety and price range of modern clubs made from moulded plastic. You may decide to buy fluorescent or even 'glow-in-the-dark' props (see the ultraviolet chapter on pages 86-88). It is always posible to redecorate the clubs for your swinging performance, for instance with coloured tape or ribbons on the base.

There are slim some clubs specially designed for club swinging and these will have tapered handles and round knobs, but they are otherwise the same as normal juggling clubs. The knobs should be firmly attached and rounded, if possible, since the smoothness helps prevent blisters. It is possible to buy round knobs if you decide to change the knobs on your clubs.

Length depends on long or short standard handle sizes. Long handle, approx. 52cm, short handle approx. 47cm. Weight, standard - approx. 230-280g each, lightweight 180-220g each. It takes less effort to swing with lightweight clubs, but heavier clubs will do more for fitness.

Clubs - Traditional Wooden Swinging Clubs

These were made of heavy hard wood, but are now difficult to find as they are antique props. Endurance club swinging contests used to be held. The participants would exercise for many hours with heavy clubs and be fed by their trainers! It is particularly important that the clubs are well balanced if you decide to swing with heavy clubs to build up your muscular strength. Small wooden clubs are occasionally used in health care by physiotherapists. Length: up to approx. 55-60cm, (22"-24"). Weight: dependent on the swinger's fitness - light for curing injuries or heavy for physical fitness - about 1½ lb. each for ladies and about 2 lb. each for men, and even up to 5-6 lb. each!

Clubs - Apparatus for Modern Rhythmic Gymnastic Competition

Gymnasts clubs are small in comparison to other clubs. They are made of wood or plastic and are available from specialist gymnastic suppliers and selected sports shops. Length, 40-50cm. Minimum weight, 150g each (i.e. very light). Knobs are rounded and the head diameter is 3cm.

Fire Clubs

These are crafted from wood and metal, with non-asbestos fire wick on the base and are available from reputable juggling suppliers. Fire torches tend to be longer and heavier than plastic juggling clubs and specialist swinging torches are also available. These will have smooth knobs and tapered handles but are otherwise the same as jugglers' torches. Fire swinging is fun, exciting and very entertaining, but can be dangerous. Read this book's chapter on fire performance and safety (pages 80-82) before starting to practise with fire.

Poles

Wood or aluminium broom sticks are cheap and readily available from D.I.Y. or other hardware shops. Use these, or cut lengths of hardwood dowelling or even plastic piping (which is very light and less damaging), when learning to spin poles. Length, approx. 110-125cm (4 feet), or cut to suit, depending on your height. Use poles that are on the short side if you decide to swing two poles at once. Diameter, approx 15-25mm.

I have put rubber stops on the ends of my poles since this reduces the sound made if they hit the floor.

Devil Stick

This juggling prop originated in China. As well as being twirlable by hand, more usually a central stick is tapped back and forth by two hand sticks and appears to suspended in mid air. The standard devil stick is made of wood or metal and plastic. Length is short: approx. 70cm (27"). Average weight, 225g (8oz).

American Baton

Made of an aluminium shaft with white rubber ball on the top and small tip on the bottom end. Specialist sports shops will be able to order batons. The recommended length is short.: Measure from your armpit, the arm held in a horizontal position, to the tip of your middle finger. Manufacturers tend to make their batons in even inches. If your arm length is an odd number of inches, (say 21"), buy a baton a size longer (22").

Chinese Ratan - Cane Stick Used by Peking Opera Pole Spinners

Specialist cane suppliers will be able to order lengths of Chinese ratan. This is a light, strong and flexible bamboo-like natural material, which is traditional for use in Chinese style pole spinning. Its flexibility makes kicking and other body-impact moves possible without injury. Length is a matter of taste, dependent upon your height and whether you are manipulating a single or two sticks. Diameter, approx 15-20mm.

Fire Devil Stick and Fire Pole

These props are straight lengths of wood with aluminium tubing and fire wick at each end. Fire devil sticks can be bought from juggling retailers but fire poles are still only rarely manufactured. My own fire poles are home made from aluminium broom sticks (for lightness) with fire wick secured to each end by crocodile clips. The clips were firmly tightened only after allowing the metal to warm up and expand. Because metal absorbs heat, the centre of the stick originally became too hot to handle. It is now wrapped in a plaster of Paris bandage, which has been taped over with electrical tape.

Wood is a much cooler material than metal and it will not conduct the heat produced at the flaming ends. However, the wood will burn away to charcoal unless you protect the area around the fire wick with metal tubing. Be sure to screw your fire wicks down firmly, or else they might fly off during a performance. Do not make the fire pole too long, particularly if you intend to swing two at once. I recommend between 110-130cms in length each. Follow sensible fire precautions when practising or performing with fire, as outlined in the fire performance and safety chapter (pages 80-82).

Buying Equipment

Most major towns now have specialist juggling retailers who stock a wide range of equipment. You can find your nearest shop by looking at the advertisements in the magazines listed opposite.

Taught Courses in Club Swinging and Circus Skills

Club swinging and other performance skills are taught at some juggling clubs and circus schools. In Britain, the major circus schools are:

Circus Space
United House
North Road
London
N7 9DP
Tel: (071) 700 0868

(as of June 1994)
Circus Space
Coronet Street
London
N1 6HD
Tel: (071) 613 4141

Skylight
Broadwater Centre
Smith Street
Rochdale
OL16 1HE
Tel: (0706) 50676

A list of local juggling clubs can be found in the juggling magazines:

The Catch
Moorledge Farm Cottage
Knowle Hill
Chew Magna
Bristol, UK
BS18 8TL
Tel: (0275) 332655

Kaskade,
The European Juggling Magazine,
Annastr. 7
D-65197 Wiesbaden
GERMANY
Tel: (49) 0611 425938
Fax: (49) 0611 410111

I teach circus skills at residential holiday centres around Britain as part of Cosmos weekends. These courses usually include work with fire and ultraviolet light. Contact the following centres for a programme:

Lower Shaw Farm
Old Shaw Lane
Shaw
Swindon
Wiltshire, UK
SN5 9PJ
Tel: (0793) 771080

Monkton Wyld Court
Charmouth
Bridport
Dorset, UK
DT6 6DQ
Tel: (0297) 60342

Laurieston Hall
The People Centre
Castle Douglas
S W SCOTLAND
DG7 2NB
Tel: (06445) 633

The above centres are communities with great atmosphere and whole food catering. Prices are low and there are reductions for non-wage earners.

If you would like up to date details of my taught courses in club swinging, pole spinning and other circus skills, please send a stamped address envelope to:

Anna Jillings
Cosmos Jugglers
71 Lawrence Street
York, UK
YO1 3DZ
Tel: (0904) 430472
Fax: (0904) 608972

Index of Illustrations

Index and Glossary

Alternating Time: Hands move in the same direction, but one half revolution apart, out of synch. (p.10 and Lesson 6, p. 25)

Arm Circle (full-arm or large arm circle): Wide diameter circles which pivot around the shoulder and use the solid grip. (p. 7, 14)

Backward Direction: Movement in the side vertical plane that passes through your body from your front to your back. Circles rise in front and then lower behind the body in the direction of swimming backstroke. (p. 5, 12)

Ball-and-Socket Grip: The knob of the club is the *ball* and the hand makes a *socket* with thumb and first two fingers. (p. 28)

Baton: A short wooden or metal rod which can be caught at either end. (p. 38, 90)

Beating: Making an audible sound by hitting equipment together in a controlled manner. (p. 74)

Black Light: Another name for ultraviolet light. (p. 2, 86-88)

Bulb or body: The widest part of a club. (p. 7)

Butt: The base of a juggling club. (p. 7)

Chase: See Cross Follow. (p. 42-43)

Club: A stick with one end thicker than the other, e.g. juggling clubs, golf clubs. Lightweight juggling clubs evolved from Indian clubs, which were heavy and made of wood. (p. 7, 89)

Club Swinging: Skill of directing two clubs in circular patterns around the body. (p. 3)

Combination: A compound trick formed by performing two (or many) different tricks simultaneously or in quick succession. (p. 21)

Count: The beat or rhythm of a pattern. (p. 21)

Cradle: The control position where equipment rests on the forearm, as though you were holding a baby. (p. 49, 57, 70-71)

Cross-Follow: A famous swinging move where one club exactly follows the path of the first club by a quarter of a revolution and the wrists seem to be hooked together. (p. 42-43)

Cross-Overs: A swing where the wrists cross each other at the front of the body. (p. 41)

Curl: Patterns which spiral in a figure 8 under-arm. (p. 49-51)

Devil Stick (or flower stick): An Oriental form of gyroscopic juggling in which a baton is juggled using short sticks to replace the hands. The central stick is tapped back and forth by two hand sticks and appears to be suspended in mid air. (p. 38, 90)

Double Time: All circles are repeated twice. (p. 22)

Drop: A prop that falls out of a pattern and onto the floor.

Elbow Circle: Medium sized circles which pivot around the elbow. (p. 19)

Figure 8: Pattern made by combining two circles of the same size into a continuous loop. (p. 30, 37, 40)

Fire Swinging: Club swinging with lit fire torches. The fire leaves stunning optical trails when swung at night or against a dark background. (p. 80-85).

Fluorescence (or day-glow): The property of absorbing light of short (invisible) wavelength and emitting light of longer (visible) wavelength. Props must be brightly coloured to shine up well under ultraviolet light. (p. 86-88)

Full-Arm Circle: Wide diameter circles with the shoulder at their centre. (p. 7, 12-13)

Follow Hand: In follow-time, the subdominant hand which chases the lead hand. (p. 42-43)

Follow Time: Usually with a figure 8 pattern, one club leads and the other follows so that clubs stay half a circle apart at all times. (p. 42, 45-46)

Forward Direction: Movement in the vertical plane that passes through your body from your front to your back. Circles fall at the front and then rise behind the body as happens when performing a swimming stroke known as "the crawl". (p. 5, 12)

Fountain: Complex pattern with changes between forward and backward cross-follows. The full-fountain consists of 6 circles swung with each hand in a circle around the body. (p. 66-69)

Front Propeller: Pole spinning pattern with a circular two handed spin in the vertical plane directly in front of the body. (p. 72)

Front Vertical Plane (or wall pane): Imaginary, flat, perpendicular surface directly in front, upright and at right angles to the horizon. (p. 9, 12)

Half Snake: Only the first, or last, part of a complete snake is performed, shortening the length of the snake movement to two circles instead of three. (p. 54-55)

Hand Circle: Small sized circles which pivot around the wrist. (p. 15)

Handle (or neck, shaft): The long, narrow part of a club. (p. 7)

Helicopter: Flat spin made on the horizontal plane, parallel to the floor. (p. 38)

Hip Snake: Snakes performed with the arms hanging down by the sides so that the clubs wrap around the forearms at hip level. (p. 56, 61)

Horizontal Plane: Imaginary flat surface, parallel to the floor and horizon. (p. 36)

Indian Clubs: Heavy wooden pins, shaped like modern juggling clubs, traditionally used for swinging, e.g. in the nineteenth century.

Inward Direction: Direction usually on the vertical plane parallel to that between your shoulders. From start position with hands at chest level, the arms rise in towards the mid line of the body (left hand rises to the right and the right hand moves up and left). On the horizontal plane, inward circles move towards the mid line of your body after they peak. (p. 6, 10-11)

Juggle: An act of dexterity and manipulation; to toss, hold, balance, handle or manipulate objects skillfully. The most popular juggling pattern is the cascade with 3 objects thrown and caught while moving in a figure of eight motion between the hands. (p. 73)

Juggling Clubs: Usually made from plastic and designed to have a balanced spin when tossed. Also used for club swinging. (p. 7, 89)

Knob: The small, rounded end of a club. (p. 7)

Lead Hand: The hand dominating the direction of a trick. In follow time, the first hand taking the move. (p. 42-43)

Luminous (or glow-in-the-dark): Material able to take in and store light which is then released over a period of time. (p. 86-88)

Mid line: Imaginary line exactly dividing the body into two symmetrical halves. It cuts between the eyes, through the nose and the tummy button and between the legs.

Modern Rhythmic Gymnastics: An Olympic sport and discipline in which women gracefully manipulate objects (including very lightweight clubs) whilst performing gymnastics in time to music. (p. 1)

Move (or trick): An action, feat or series of repetitive motions learned as a result of practise.

Outward Direction: Movements usually in a plane that is parallel to that between your shoulders. Clubs move from the centre of the body (in starting position, p. 8) and go towards the outside of the body. On the horizontal plane, outward circles are those moving out from the mid line to the outside of the body. (p. 6, 9, 11)

Opposition Time: One side rotates circles forward, whilst at the same time the other spins backward. (p. 14, 17)

Parallel: Hands move together, continually side by side. One hand takes one direction, and the other follows its path so that clubs remain the same distance apart at all points. Parallel moves can go left or right. (p. 11, 45-48)

Pattern: The path props follow in the swing or juggle.

Pendulum: A move that is not circular. Instead there is a half swing from side to side, like the motion of a see-saw. (p. 48)

Pirouette: A 360-degree turn executed by the performer. (p. 14)

Placement: Instead of being held always in the hand, the equipment is placed to rest for a moment on some part of the body, e.g. under the knee, on the shoulder. (p. 74)

Pole Spinning: The action of rotating a stick (such as a broom stick) to spin in circular patterns. (p. 27, 38, 40, 70-72)

Popular Reel: Outward, combination full-arm and shoulder circles in alternating time. (p. 25)

Reel: A class of club swinging patterns in alternating time, usually on the front vertical plane. (p. 25, 31)

Ring Grip: A grip in which a ring is made around the club knob by thumb and forefinger, allowing the knob enough play to rotate freely. (p. 15)

Rolling: Pushing the equipment off to make a circle on the floor. (p. 74)

Routine: Moves that are put together in a set order. (p. 11, 24, 41, 78-79, 83-85)

Side Vertical Plane: Imaginary flat surface running parallel to the mid line from the front to the back of the body. It is perpendicular to the horizon and contains the forward and backward directions. (p. 12)

Single Ratio Movements: Where patterns are made with only a single circumference.

Short Reel: Alternating time lower-front and back hand circles on the front vertical plane. (p. 31)

Shoulder Circle (or upper-back circle): Hand sized circles made slightly behind the shoulder. (p. 19)

Snake: The clubs coil around the forearms, being the part of the arm from the elbow to the wrist. Lessons 13 - 16 are devoted to snake moves (p. 49-61).

Snake Grip: Grip used for snake movements with the club grasped by its neck and with the forefinger over the knob to steady the grip. (p. 49)

Solid Grip: Strong grip on the club with the knob held between the thumb and first two fingers. (p. 7)

Starting Position: Basic standing position in a closed stance with the clubs held straight upright in front at chest level and with arms slightly bent. (p. 8)

Swinger: Person who enjoys club swinging. (p. 1)

Symmetry: Correct proportion of the parts of a pattern giving balance, harmony and beauty.

Synchronous Time: Both hands move, at the same time, simultaneously in a single direction. (p. 9, 11)

Throwing Hand: The hand from which a thrown object originates.

Torches: Fire clubs for fire swinging or fire juggling. (p. 80-82, 89)

Trail: Path line taken by a club. When club swinging the trails are usually circular.

Transition: A planned change from one move to another in a routine, Lesson 8 (p. 33)

Tray Plane: The level horizontal plane in which a flat swing moves. It is parallel to the floor and horizon (e.g. a helicopter spin). (p. 36, 38)

Trick: In juggling or club swinging (for instance), any single manipulation or combination of moves performed ostensibly for the entertainment of an audience or for personal amusement.

Ultraviolet Light (or black light): UV is a light frequency that enhances fluorescent equipment. Club swinging under uv is extremely effective as the special lighting emphasizes the moving patterns of the clubs. (p. 2, 86-88)

Vertical Plane (see wall plane)

Waist Wrap: Follow-time pattern circling around the waist. (p. 62-66)

Wall Plane (or vertical plane): Imaginary perpendicular surface within which certain swinging moves are supposed to stay. The most used vertical planes are: a) parallel to the planes either directly in front, or behind the body; or b) at right angles to the first plane, parallel with the mid line of your body between the eyes down through the nose. (p. 12)

References

Books

Club Swinging for Physical Exercise and Recreation by W J Schatz. Published by Brian Dube Inc. Reprinted from a volume published in 1908 by the American Gymnasia Co.

Juggling with Finesse by Kit Summers. Published by Finesse Press, 1987.

Modern Rhythmic Gymnastics by Jenny Bott. Published by EP Publishing Limited, in the EP Sport series 1981.

Contact Juggling by James Ernest. Published by Ernest Graphics Press 1990.

Baton Twirling - The Fundamentals of an Art and a Skill by Constance Atwater. Published by the Charles E Tuttle Company, Inc. 1964.

Research on Clubs and Sticks by John Bolwell including:
      a) **Comprehensive Asian Fighting Arts** by Dan F Draeger & Robert W Smith.
      b) **The Way of the Warrior** by Howard Reid & Michael Croucher.
      c) **The Devil Stick Book** by Todd Strong.
      d) **The Mystic Spiral** by Jill Purce.

Video

Club Swinging by Allan Jacobs. Maverick Media / IJA Productions 1990.

Magazines

Kaskade, European Juggling Magazine. Published by Gabi and Paul Keast, Annastr.7, D-65197, Wiesbaden, Germany.

The Catch, British Juggling Magazine. Published by Jan and Stuart Ashman, Moorledge Farm Cottage, Knowle Hill, Chew Magna, Bristol, BS18 8TL, England.

photographer Simon Heathfield

About the Author

Since her performing career began in 1991 with the Oxford fire troupe 'FireNoise', Anna Jillings has developed a graceful style which has made her one of Europe's best known club swingers.

Anna has appeared in the public shows of the major British and European Juggling conventions and performs at cabaret and theatre venues as far afield as Thailand. She has a continually evolving solo show as well as a partnership in the York based juggling group 'Cosmos'.

Anna writes as the British Correspondent to the European Juggling Magazine 'Kaskade'.

Her experience teaching one day and residential courses in club swinging and other manipulative arts to people of all ages forms the core of the lessons presented in this book.